Self Love Book for Men

CRAFTED BY SKRIUWER

Copyright © 2024 by Skriuwer.

All rights reserved. No part of this book may be used or reproduced in any form whatsoever without written permission except in the case of brief quotations in critical articles or reviews.

For more information, contact : **kontakt@skriuwer.com** (www.skriuwer.com)

TABLE OF CONTENTS

CHAPTER 1: THE MEANING OF SELF RESPECT

- How self respect differs from arrogance
- Common signals of missing self respect
- Practical steps for building a stable sense of worth

CHAPTER 2: BREAKING OLD BELIEFS

- Identifying harmful thoughts from the past
- Replacing outdated ideas with more helpful ones
- Steady ways to challenge unhelpful beliefs

CHAPTER 3: POSITIVE THOUGHTS FOR DAILY LIFE

- Simple methods to shift negative self-talk
- Using mindfulness for calm and focus
- Daily exercises to grow a more optimistic viewpoint

CHAPTER 4: BUILDING INNER STRENGTH

- Finding clear personal values to guide actions
- Using self-discipline without feeling rigid
- Recognizing weakness and turning it into growth

CHAPTER 5: STEPS TO HANDLE EMOTIONAL PAIN

- Identifying signs of deeper sorrow
- Safe outlets for expressing strong feelings
- How to seek help without shame

CHAPTER 6: DISCOVERING PERSONAL INTERESTS

- *Brainstorming ways to find what lights you up*
- *Handling worries about looking silly or failing*
- *Balancing new hobbies with responsibilities*

CHAPTER 7: TACTICS FOR A HEALTHY LIFESTYLE

- *Nutrition basics that support body and mind*
- *Fitting exercise into busy schedules*
- *Practical tools for handling stress and rest*

CHAPTER 8: TRUE FRIENDSHIPS AND CONNECTION

- *Building genuine bonds through trust*
- *Avoiding shallow talk to form deeper links*
- *Conflict resolution skills that keep friendships strong*

CHAPTER 9: BUILDING A PRODUCTIVE MINDSET

- *Clear goal-setting and breaking large tasks down*
- *Time-blocking and handling distractions*
- *Practical methods to avoid burnout*

CHAPTER 10: SKILLS FOR GOOD COMMUNICATION

- *Speaking honestly but respectfully*
- *Active listening for stronger understanding*
- *Solving conflicts and reducing misunderstandings*

CHAPTER 11: MANAGING CONFLICT AT WORK & HOME

- *Recognizing common causes of disputes*
- *Using calm, fair methods to solve disagreements*
- *Preventing small problems from growing larger*

CHAPTER 12: OVERCOMING SHAME AND GUILT

- *Distinguishing between guilt over actions and shame at the core*
- *Healthy ways to process regret and move on*
- *Stopping negative cycles of self-criticism*

CHAPTER 13: ACHIEVING PERSONAL GOALS

- *Breaking aims into clear, reachable steps*
- *Tracking progress and adjusting plans sensibly*
- *Staying motivated when results take time*

CHAPTER 14: GROWTH THROUGH REFLECTION

- *Developing a habit of looking inward*
- *Using journals or mindful breaks to gain insight*
- *Turning lessons learned into real daily changes*

CHAPTER 15: PRACTICAL WAYS TO FIND MOTIVATION

- *Connecting tasks to deeper values*
- *Setting up supportive partners or groups*
- *Handling slumps with small, steady actions*

CHAPTER 16: HANDLING STRESS WITHOUT HARM

- Spotting early signs of tension before burnout
- Combining quick fixes and long-term healthy practices
- Knowing when to seek professional help

CHAPTER 17: BALANCING PERSONAL NEEDS AND RELATIONSHIPS

- Setting fair limits to protect personal space
- Dividing home tasks and duties for harmony
- Finding ways to nurture both yourself and loved ones

CHAPTER 18: CREATING A SUPPORT NETWORK

- Building trust with friends, mentors, and helpful groups
- Offering support as much as you receive it
- Overcoming social anxieties or past letdowns

CHAPTER 19: LONG-TERM PLANS FOR WELL-BEING

- Sustaining good habits through life's changes
- Scheduling periodic checkups and personal audits
- Staying adaptable as goals and situations evolve

CHAPTER 20: CONCLUSION AND FINAL THOUGHTS

- Bringing together all the core lessons
- Emphasizing daily consistency and self-compassion
- Charting your path forward with openness and care

CHAPTER 1

The Meaning of Self Respect

Introduction

Self respect may sound like a simple idea, but it holds a strong place in a man's life. It is about looking at yourself in the mirror and feeling worthy. It is about staying true to your own rules and personal code. It is about treating your physical and mental needs in a fair and caring way. Some people confuse self respect with being self-centered, but these two are not the same. A self-centered person might only think about his needs and ignore the needs of others. A man who has self respect knows that he must consider himself in a balanced way. He knows he must not ignore his own needs, but he also should not forget about others.

In this chapter, we will look at the idea of self respect in several ways. First, we will learn why self respect is more than just liking yourself. Then, we will discuss the effect self respect has on relationships, work, and even physical health. We will also discuss how a man can notice if his sense of self respect is too low or too high. Finally, we will look at how to start growing a true sense of self respect without stepping on others.

1.1 Self Respect Is Not Arrogance

Some men confuse self respect with bragging or showing off. That is a common misunderstanding. Self respect means understanding your strengths but also being aware of your limits. For example, a man might be good at his job, but he realizes that he needs help from others to reach certain goals. He does not act like he knows it all. Instead, he stays open to learning new skills. That man is practicing true self respect because he is being honest with himself.

Arrogance, on the other hand, often masks a lack of self respect. When a person brags too much, it can show that he feels uncertain on the inside. He tries to cover that feeling by telling others how great he is. But deep inside, he might be worried that he is not good enough. So, when we talk about self respect in this book, we do not mean puffing ourselves up. We mean having a calm understanding that we have value, while also knowing there is room to grow.

1.2 Signs of Missing Self Respect

If a man has little self respect, it can show up in different ways. Some men might notice that they agree to everything others ask. They might fear that saying "no" will make people dislike them. This need to please can lead to feeling tired or even upset. Over time, this man may lose sight of what he wants because he is so used to doing what others want.

Another sign of low self respect is never giving time or space for personal needs. For example, a man might never take care of his health or never stand up for himself when others treat him badly. He might think he does not deserve better. He might also put himself down with words like, "I cannot do anything right," or "I am not as good as them." Constant negative self-talk can tear down a man's sense of self, making it hard for him to see any of his good qualities.

When self respect is missing, it can also affect relationships. One person might depend too much on a friend or romantic partner for approval. He might worry nonstop about losing that person because he believes he is not good enough. This worry can cause stress and lead to unhealthy patterns.

1.3 Benefits of Having Healthy Self Respect

Men who have a balanced sense of self respect tend to set fair boundaries. They know what they are willing to accept from others and where they must draw a line. This helps them create healthy relationships because they do not let others take advantage of them. It also helps them at work, where they can speak up about problems or needs in a confident way.

Healthy self respect can also improve mental well-being. By trusting in your own value, you are less likely to fall into harmful self-criticism. You might be able to handle tough situations without feeling hopeless. Instead, you might see these challenges as problems you can solve or lessons you can learn.

A man with self respect also tends to take better care of his physical health. He might choose better foods, try to get enough sleep, and seek regular checkups. He does these things not because he wants to show off, but because he understands that his body needs proper care.

1.4 The Difference Between High Self Esteem and Self Respect

Some folks see self respect and self esteem as the same idea. While they are related, there is a slight difference. Self esteem often deals with how you rate yourself, including how capable or skilled you think you are. Self respect includes how you treat yourself as a person, beyond just skills.

A man might feel high self esteem when he is good at sports or business, yet he could still have low self respect if he ignores his need for rest. Another man might not be the best performer at work, but he still respects himself enough to eat well, exercise, and speak kindly to himself.

1.5 Building Self Respect Through Small Choices

Growth often starts with small choices. For example, deciding to say "no" when you really cannot take on another task is an act of self respect. It shows that you value your own limits and are not afraid to stand by them. Another small choice might be to speak calmly in a heated argument instead of letting anger take over. When you choose to respond in a way that lines up with your values, you are acting with self respect.

Small choices can also look like grooming yourself well each morning, not out of vanity, but because you want to present yourself in a dignified way. It might also mean taking time to reflect on your daily wins, no matter how small they are. Doing so can help you see that you matter and that your efforts are worth it.

1.6 Handling Criticism

Part of a strong sense of self respect is being able to handle criticism without falling apart. When someone points out a mistake, a man with balanced self respect can say, "Thank you for pointing that out. I will see how I can fix it." He does not see the mistake as proof that he is worthless. Instead, he views it as a chance to learn or improve. He does not feel angry at the person giving the feedback, because he understands that no one is perfect.

On the flip side, if the criticism is unfair or rude, a man with good self respect can calmly say, "I feel this is not fair" or "I think we should talk about the details," without lashing out or running away. He knows it is okay to stand up for himself when needed.

1.7 Recognizing Personal Accomplishments

Many men focus on what they have not done yet. They push themselves to keep trying harder. While striving for goals is good, it is also important to see what you have already done. Recognizing your accomplishments, whether big or small, helps you see your worth. This can be as simple as recalling the time you helped a friend move to a new home, or the time you overcame a personal setback. By recalling these events, you remind yourself that you are capable.

1.8 Respecting Others While Respecting Yourself

Some men think that respecting themselves means they might ignore others. That does not have to happen. Real self respect teaches you to appreciate others while also standing up for your own needs. You can offer kindness to others without letting them walk all over you. For instance, if a friend keeps borrowing your car and returning it with no gas, you can say, "I am happy to help, but please fill up the tank." You are not pushing your friend away, you are just setting a fair condition.

1.9 How Society Shapes Self Respect in Men

In many cultures, men are expected to be strong, never cry, and never show doubt. These expectations can cause men to hide their struggles. Some men might think that if they admit to needing help, they are less manly. Over time, this can lower self respect because they might neglect their own well-being, all to maintain a tough image.

It helps to question these social norms. Real strength is not about hiding pain, but about dealing with it in a sensible way. Sometimes that means talking to a friend or even a professional when you face challenges. That is an act of self respect because you are caring for your own mind.

1.10 A Real Example of Self Respect in Action

Consider a man who was always told he was not "manly" enough. He felt pressured to act tough. He might have forced himself to hide his gentle nature. Over time, he felt fake and unhappy. One day, he realized he should not ignore his real self. He started to show his kindness openly. He also learned to say "no" when people teased him or tried to make him feel small. As he practiced being his real self, he noticed he had more genuine friends. His self respect grew because he was honoring who he truly was.

1.11 Self Respect at Work

At work, self respect may show up in the way you present your ideas. A person with low self respect might shy away from giving input in a meeting, even if he has a valuable opinion. He might worry that he is not smart enough or that others will judge him. Meanwhile, a person with balanced self respect will speak up politely, but firmly. He does not yell or talk over others, but he also does not hide from sharing what he believes.

Additionally, self respect can affect how you handle tasks. If you respect yourself, you are more likely to do tasks with care. You are also more likely to be honest when you cannot meet a deadline. Hiding mistakes or problems only leads to bigger issues. Being upfront is a sign that you value yourself and the work you do.

1.12 Practical Ways to Strengthen Self Respect

- **Set clear limits**: Know what you can handle each day. If you are too busy, politely turn down extra tasks.
- **Speak kindly to yourself**: Watch out for negative self-talk. Replace phrases like "I am a failure" with "I made a mistake, but I can learn."
- **Keep promises you make to yourself**: If you say you will exercise three times a week, stick to it. Not keeping your own promises can erode self respect.
- **Allow yourself to rest**: Men often push themselves non-stop. Recognize that rest is a need, not a weakness.
- **Ask for help when needed**: This does not show weakness. It shows you value your well-being enough to get support.

1.13 Knowing When You Are Moving in the Right Direction

You will know that your self respect is growing when you notice changes in how you feel daily. For instance, you might stop second-guessing yourself when deciding what to eat or wear. You might feel less stressed about what others think. You might find yourself looking forward to new challenges at work because you see them as interesting rather than scary. These small signs point to an increase in self respect.

1.14 Avoiding Pitfalls

One common pitfall is comparing yourself to others. Everyone is on a different timeline, and each person has different strengths and weaknesses. Constant comparison can make you feel bad, even if you have done a lot. Focus on your own progress and how you can improve on your own terms.

Another pitfall is ignoring self respect in an attempt to please everyone. Trying to make everyone like you is impossible. Instead, aim to treat others with fairness while also treating yourself with the same fairness.

1.15 Taking It Day by Day

Building self respect is not a quick fix. It takes daily practice. One helpful tip is to keep a small notebook and jot down moments in the day when you showed respect for yourself. Maybe you said, "No, I cannot help you tonight," because you had already made a promise to yourself to rest. Or maybe you chose to turn off your phone for a short break when you felt overwhelmed. These small notes can serve as proof that you are on the right path.

1.16 Final Thoughts on Self Respect

Self respect is a key part of a man's sense of worth. It involves honest self-awareness, reasonable boundaries, and a willingness to stand by your own needs while staying aware of the needs of others. It protects you from letting external pressures shape your life. It also allows you to stay steady in tough times, instead of feeling small or out of control.

By noticing signs of missing self respect and taking simple steps to grow a healthier sense of self, men can lead more balanced lives. In the next chapter, we will look at how old beliefs can block self respect. We will also discuss how to break these old patterns so you can continue growing.

CHAPTER 2

Breaking Old Beliefs

Introduction

Many men carry old beliefs that can hold them back. These might include thoughts like, "I must always win to be respected," or "I cannot show any weakness," or even "I am not worth much." These beliefs often start in childhood or early adulthood. They can come from family, community, or personal experiences. Over time, these beliefs can shape how you see yourself, how you act at work, and how you treat your friends and loved ones.

In this chapter, we will explore ways men can identify and challenge harmful old beliefs. We will also talk about how to replace them with more helpful perspectives. We will look at some real-life examples of men who have managed to let go of these blocks. At the end of this chapter, you will have practical steps to unlearn unhelpful ideas and welcome more accurate ways of thinking.

2.1 Understanding Where Old Beliefs Come From

Men might develop specific beliefs because of how they grew up. Maybe you were told by a parent, "Real men never cry." Over time, you accepted that statement as truth. Now you might feel guilty or ashamed any time a tear forms in your eye. Another common source of old beliefs is personal trauma or hardship. If you failed at a major goal, you might start to think, "I am a failure in everything." This single event can begin to affect your entire sense of self.

Media can also push certain beliefs. For example, movies might show men who always fix problems without asking for help. This can lead some men to think that asking for help is a sign of weakness. Over time, such beliefs can become so strong that men do not realize they are even there. They might think, "That is just how life is."

2.2 The Impact of Unhelpful Beliefs

When old beliefs are not helpful, they can cause many problems. A man who thinks he must never show weakness might have trouble opening up to his partner or friends. He might hide his problems and feel lonely. Another man might think he has no value, so he never pursues better jobs or tries to reach new goals. He might remain stuck in a place that does not reflect his true ability.

These beliefs can also cause stress. For instance, trying to appear perfect all the time is exhausting. Sooner or later, cracks will appear, and the man might face burnout. Another source of stress comes from the conflict between reality and the old belief. If you believe "a real man always knows the right answers," but then you find yourself confused at work, you experience a clash that can cause anxiety or shame.

2.3 Spotting Your Old Beliefs

To challenge old beliefs, you first need to spot them. Here are some ways you can try:

1. **Write down your main thoughts**: Spend a few minutes each day writing what you say to yourself. Notice any common patterns.
2. **Pay attention to strong emotions**: When you feel intense anger, fear, or sadness, ask yourself, "What idea might be causing this reaction?"
3. **Ask people who know you well**: Sometimes friends or family see patterns that you might miss. You can ask, "Have you noticed any beliefs I have about myself or life that do not seem accurate?"

These steps might feel uncomfortable, but they can open your eyes to ideas that run under your daily thoughts. You do not have to accept every piece of feedback from others, but consider it if it shows up repeatedly.

2.4 Challenging Old Beliefs

Once you spot an old belief, the next step is to test it. This can be done through self-talk or even writing exercises. For example, if your old belief is "I always mess up," gather proof that this is not true. Maybe you do well in certain tasks at work or home. Maybe you once solved a big problem for a friend. List these successes. When the negative belief pops up, you can look at that list.

It might also help to question where the belief started. If your dad once said something hurtful, ask yourself if what he said was based on real fact or just his personal opinion. Understanding the source of a belief can help you see that it may not be a universal truth.

2.5 Replacing Old Beliefs with More Fair Ones

Challenging a belief is not enough. You need to replace it with a new thought pattern. For instance, if your old belief was "I must always be tough," replace it with, "It is okay to feel sad or worried sometimes, and it does not make me less of a man." Repeating this statement to yourself can help shape your new mindset. It will take time before this new thought feels comfortable. Old habits tend to linger, but consistency can create lasting change.

2.6 Handling Pushback from Others

When you start changing your beliefs, people around you might be surprised. If you used to always play the tough guy, your friends might tease you if they notice you being more open about your struggles. This can be uncomfortable, but it is part of the process. You might gently tell them, "I am learning to be more honest about my feelings." You do not have to convince them. Over time, if they care about you, they will accept this change.

2.7 Real-Life Example: Mark's Story

Mark grew up in a home where his mother often said, "Boys do not cry." When Mark was in his teens, he hurt his ankle badly, but he still tried not to show any tears. As an adult, he carried the belief that he should never feel weak. This caused him to hide his struggles from his wife, which led to arguments. She felt he was shutting her out. One day, Mark decided to question where his unwillingness to show sadness came from. He realized it traced back to that old phrase from his mother. He began telling himself, "Feeling sad does not make me less strong." After a few months of practice, he found it easier to share tough feelings with his wife. Their relationship improved, and Mark noticed he felt more at peace.

2.8 The Role of Therapy and Support Groups

Some beliefs are so deep that it is hard to tackle them alone. In these cases, therapy or support groups can help. A trained counselor can guide you to see these beliefs clearly. They can offer tools to challenge them and replace them with healthier thoughts. Some men feel uneasy about going to therapy, worried about how it looks. But caring for your mental health is a sign of taking your personal needs seriously.

Support groups, whether in person or online, can also provide a place to share your struggles without feeling judged. Hearing other men talk about similar issues might help you see that your old beliefs are not unique. This can ease feelings of isolation.

2.9 Physical Actions to Help Shift Your Mindset

Sometimes, taking physical action can support mental change. For example, if your old belief says, "I cannot face conflict," you might practice role-playing conflict scenarios with a friend or therapist. If your old belief says, "I am not strong," you might start a fitness routine and track your progress. Seeing yourself get better physically can help reinforce the idea that growth is possible.

It can also help to try new things that challenge your comfort zone. If you have always avoided public speaking because you thought you would fail, trying a small local group presentation can show that your fears might not be completely accurate. Even if you make mistakes, you can still see that you are capable of growth.

2.10 How Technology Can Help

In modern times, there are apps that can help you track your thought patterns. Some allow you to record daily moods and keep track of the beliefs you are working on. You can set reminders to practice positive self-talk. There are even online forums where men discuss their old beliefs and how they are managing to let go. While technology is not a cure-all, it can offer extra support.

2.11 Seeing Challenges as Chances for Growth

When you run into a challenge that goes against your old beliefs, it can feel uncomfortable. But these moments are also good chances to test out your new thoughts. Let's say you are in a team meeting at work and you do not know the answer to a question. Your old belief might tell you, "I must have all the answers, or I look weak." Your new belief might be, "It is okay not to know everything, and it is wise to learn." In that moment, you can say, "I am not sure about that, let's find out together." This small act can break the hold of the old belief.

2.12 The Importance of Repetition

Breaking old beliefs is rarely a one-time event. Think of it like learning a new skill. If you only practice once, it does not stick. You need repeated exposure to the new belief before it becomes part of you. This may mean writing the new belief on a sticky note and placing it where you see it each day. It may mean telling yourself the new belief whenever you wake up, or when you go to bed, or whenever you notice the old belief sneaking back.

2.13 Watching Out for Hidden Beliefs

Sometimes, old beliefs are so hidden that they show up only in certain situations. You might notice it when you face a personal setback or when you start a new job. For example, you might catch yourself saying, "I am a nobody," if you fail a test. That might be a sign of a deeper belief that you are only worthy if you succeed. Being aware of these hidden beliefs can help you address them before they become bigger problems.

2.14 Shifting Your Self-Talk

Words have power, especially the words you say to yourself. If you often think, "I am useless," you might start to feel that way, even if it is not true. Shifting self-talk to something balanced can help. Instead of "I am useless," try, "I have areas where I need improvement, but I also have areas where I am good." This does not mean lying to yourself. It means being accurate. Everyone has strengths and weaknesses.

2.15 Getting Feedback from Safe People

If you are not sure how accurate your new beliefs are, you can talk to someone you trust. This can be a mentor, a close friend, or a counselor. You might say, "I am working on the idea that it is okay to show I do not know something. Does that seem reasonable to you?" Pick people who understand you and want to see you do well. Sometimes, an outside view helps confirm that you are on the right path.

2.16 Knowing When to Let Go

There might be people in your life who reinforce your old beliefs. For example, if you are trying to let go of the idea "I must act tough 24/7," but you have a friend who mocks you whenever you open up, that person is making your work harder. In some cases, you might need to limit contact with such people or clearly tell them, "I am changing how I view myself, and I would appreciate your support." If they do not respect that, it might be time to reconsider if you want them around.

2.17 A Quick Exercise

Try this short exercise to begin reshaping old beliefs:

1. Write down an old belief that bothers you, such as "I am not good enough."

2. Write down proof that goes against this belief. For instance, "I learned a new skill last month" or "I helped my teammate solve a problem."
3. Write a new statement that feels more accurate, such as "I have room to grow, but I am doing better than I realize."
4. Read this new statement every morning for a week. Notice any shifts in how you feel over time.

This exercise helps rewire the mind to see facts rather than old assumptions.

2.18 Life Beyond Old Beliefs

When men release old, harmful beliefs, life can open up. You might find new ways to handle relationships, new motivation at work, and an overall better state of mind. You can also approach problems with a flexible mindset, because you no longer see them as proof that you are inadequate, but as a natural part of living.

2.19 How This Chapter Links to Self Respect

Self respect and old beliefs are linked. It is hard to respect yourself if you are carrying beliefs that tear you down or that hold impossible standards over your head. By challenging and changing these beliefs, you allow yourself to see your own worth more clearly. You also free yourself to take better care of your needs.

2.20 Final Thoughts on Breaking Old Beliefs

Rewriting old beliefs takes time, patience, and courage. The key steps are spotting them, challenging them with facts, and then replacing them with more balanced ideas. Support from counselors, friends, or family can make this process easier. Technology and exercises can also help you stay on track.

Letting go of what is unhelpful in your mind is an important step toward a healthier sense of self. In the next chapter, we will look at the power of positive thoughts in daily life. We will dig into practical ways to replace negative self-talk and keep a strong and balanced mindset.

CHAPTER 3

Positive Thoughts for Daily Life

Introduction
Every day, we have many thoughts passing through our minds. Some thoughts are helpful, while others can make us feel bad. Men often deal with stress from work, family duties, and social expectations. All of these responsibilities can lead to worries, self-criticism, or irritations. For some men, these troublesome thoughts add up until it feels overwhelming. However, there is a way to reduce the weight of these thoughts: learn to shape your thinking patterns in a more balanced and clear way.

This does not mean that you force yourself to only think about bright, happy things. Life has real challenges, and ignoring them will not help. Instead, positive thoughts involve noticing both the good and the not-so-good, and choosing to focus on solutions, hope, and acceptance of reality rather than endless worry. This chapter will look at how men can reshape their thinking patterns day to day. We will explore common traps that lead to negative feelings and practical ways to build a healthy mindset that supports you.

3.1 The Mind's Tendency to Focus on Negatives

Our minds are wired to look for problems. This is a survival trait left over from ancient times when people had to stay aware of threats. This survival tactic can still be helpful in modern life, but it also means we often notice the bad things more than the good things. For example, if ten good events happen and one bad event occurs, many people will fixate on the one bad event. This can lead to feeling like life is worse than it really is.

By recognizing this tendency, you can start to notice when your mind is going on a "negative loop." For example, if you find yourself thinking about a small mistake you made last week for hours, you can pause and remind yourself that dwelling on it is not fixing anything. This step of noticing is key to stopping a negative chain of thoughts. Once you are aware, you can do something different, like shifting your attention to a solution or a more balanced perspective.

3.2 Why Positive Thoughts Matter

A man's thought patterns can influence how he feels about himself. If your mind is always pointing out faults, you may begin to feel hopeless. You may also lose motivation to try new activities because you keep telling yourself that you will fail. On the other hand, when your mind is trained to look for possible solutions or see the good in a tough situation, you are more likely to keep going and find success over time.

Positive thoughts also affect how you treat others. If you consistently see the bad in your coworkers or friends, you might act defensive or angry. But if you focus on the fact that most people have some good traits, you can approach them with more understanding. This does not mean ignoring problems. Instead, it means training your mind to see a fuller picture, one that includes any positive detail that might help you handle the situation.

3.3 Myths about Positive Thinking

Some people think that positive thinking means wearing a fake smile all day. That is a misunderstanding. Real positive thinking allows for sadness, frustration, and disappointment. It simply does not let these feelings become the entire story. Rather than denying problems, you acknowledge them and then ask, "What can I learn here? Is there any small benefit I can notice?"

Another myth is that positive thinking will solve everything instantly. Even the best mindset cannot erase real-life issues on its own. You still need to take action, make plans, and sometimes seek help from others. Positive thinking gives you the foundation to tackle life with an even mind, but it does not remove the need for work or responsibility.

A third myth is that you must be "born" a positive person. While some individuals seem more cheerful from birth, many men who have become quite positive had to practice. They had to learn how to talk to themselves in a supportive way. If you feel you lean toward negativity, it does not mean you are stuck there.

3.4 Building a Supportive Inner Voice

An inner voice is the way you talk to yourself in your head. This voice can be harsh or supportive, sometimes both. Some men picked up a harsh inner voice from hearing lots of criticism while growing up. Others formed a gentle inner voice by being around encouraging people. If you notice that your inner voice is mostly negative, you can work on changing it.

1. **Identify the harsh messages**: Listen for times you might say, "I am an idiot," or "I always fail." Write these messages down.
2. **Question them**: Ask yourself, "Is it true that I always fail? What about the times I succeeded?"
3. **Add balance**: Replace extreme phrases with balanced ones like, "I made a mistake, but I can fix it," or "I might not be perfect, but I can learn."

Over time, these new messages can become your normal way of talking to yourself. This helps in both calm days and tough days because your mind will be ready to help you, not tear you down.

3.5 Specific Techniques for Thinking in a Healthier Way

- **Daily Reflections**: Spend a few minutes each evening or morning thinking about what went well the day before. This can be as simple as enjoying a good meal or finishing a small task at work. By shining a light on positive events, you teach your brain to notice good things more.
- **Choosing Your Words Carefully**: Even words said jokingly can shape your mindset. If you call yourself "dumb" or "hopeless" as a joke, your brain still picks up on that negativity. Try to use words that are fair or at least neutral, such as "I made an error," instead of "I am useless."
- **Focus on Solutions**: When a problem arises, shift your mind to possible fixes rather than the problem itself. For example, if you are late to work because of traffic, you could plan an earlier commute next time, or see if public transport is an option. This approach trains your brain to look for actions you can take rather than staying stuck.

3.6 Mindfulness for Daily Life

Mindfulness is a simple practice of being present. It means focusing on the current moment, instead of replaying the past or panicking about the future. One way to start mindfulness is to notice small details around you: the sound of birds, the feeling of your chair, or the taste of your drink. This might seem unimportant, but it helps calm a busy brain.

When your mind is calmer, it is easier to think positive thoughts because you are not caught up in a whirl of worries. You might find that when you give full attention to an activity, such as washing dishes or walking your dog, you feel less stressed. This can make space for clearer thinking. Over time, mindfulness can help you observe your own patterns of thought with more understanding.

3.7 The Power of People Around You

Your circle of friends, coworkers, and family can either boost or drain your thinking. If you are often around people who are always putting you down or painting life in a hopeless manner, it can be harder to stay balanced. You do not always get to pick who is in your environment, like coworkers or certain family members. However, you can choose how much power their words have over you.

You might set small limits. For example, if a coworker constantly rants about everything, you can limit how often you chat with them about negative topics. Instead, try to steer the conversation to something productive. If you have a friend who constantly mocks you, you can calmly say that you would like them to stop. You have the right to protect your mindset. In an ideal situation, you also find supportive people who encourage your efforts to have a more positive outlook.

3.8 Balancing Hope with Realism

Some men worry that thinking too positively is naive. They fear they will overlook problems or appear foolish. The key is balancing hope with realism. You do not say, "Everything is fine," when it is not. Instead, you acknowledge issues, but also remind yourself that life is not hopeless. You might say, "This is going to be hard, but I can figure it out," or, "I am worried, but I will not give up before I try."

In situations like a lost job or a broken relationship, positive thinking will not take away the sadness instantly. But it can keep you from blaming yourself entirely or sinking into despair. It can also help you take useful steps. For instance, if you lose a job, instead of telling yourself you will never work again, you can think, "I am sad, but I will update my resume and look for new places to apply."

3.9 Handling Negativity without Denial

Negative thoughts can sometimes be signals. They might alert you to a real threat or a genuine area in your life that needs fixing. For instance, feeling uneasy about your finances may be a hint that you need to create a budget. In that sense, negativity can serve a purpose, as long as you do not let it spiral into hopelessness.

This means that you do not have to push away all negative feelings as soon as they pop up. Instead, you notice them, figure out if they are pointing to a real issue, and then do something about it if needed. This approach turns negativity into a small alarm bell rather than a prison that holds you back.

3.10 Helpful Questions to Ask Yourself

Sometimes, guiding your mind with good questions can shift your perspective. Here are a few examples:

1. **"Is there a piece of this situation I can control?"**
   If you can identify even one small part you can manage, you stop feeling like everything is out of your hands.
2. **"Is there another way to view this situation?"**
   You might be focusing only on one angle. Try to see if there is another angle that is less upsetting or more fair.
3. **"Will this matter one year from now?"**
   Many daily worries that weigh us down do not matter in the long run. This question can put things in perspective.

4. **"What steps can I take to feel better or fix the problem?"**
   Shifting your brain from worry to action can help break negativity.

3.11 Keeping a Thought Journal

A thought journal is a place to write down your repetitive thoughts. It can be a notebook, a file on your phone, or any method that feels comfortable. The process is straightforward: when you notice a strong negative or anxious thought, jot it down. Then, write what was happening at that moment and how you felt in your body.

Next, look at what you wrote and try to find a more balanced statement. For example, if you wrote, "I messed up this project, I am hopeless," you might note a balanced version like, "I made an error, but I learned from it, and I can try again." Keeping this journal for a few weeks can help you see patterns in your thinking. You might spot triggers—people, places, or times of day that make negative thoughts more likely. This knowledge can help you prepare solutions or coping strategies.

3.12 Real Stories of Positive Thought in Action

1. **Carlos**: Carlos always felt that people at work were judging him. He believed he was not good enough because he once forgot an important deadline. He started noticing how often he assumed others were looking down on him. He wrote these thoughts in a small notebook. Over time, he saw that this belief was not based on real proof—none of his coworkers had actually said anything negative to him. By replacing this assumption with, "They see me as a normal coworker," Carlos felt more relaxed and started contributing more ideas in meetings.
2. **Sam**: Sam had grown used to telling himself, "I am no good at talking to people." This made him dread social events. One day, he decided to try a small experiment. He told himself, "I can at least say hello and ask one question," every time he met someone new. After a few tries, Sam noticed that people were actually polite and sometimes eager to talk. This changed his self-talk to, "I might not be the best speaker, but I can hold a friendly chat." This small step toward a more helpful thought made him feel less anxious and more open to meeting new people.

3.13 Overcoming Common Obstacles to Positive Thinking

- **Habit of Criticism**: If you have spent years thinking negatively, it feels normal. Breaking this habit takes time. Do not expect a complete shift overnight. Instead, celebrate small improvements in your thought patterns (note the use of "recognize" rather than a certain word you wanted to avoid).
- **Toxic Environments**: You might have a boss who is always criticizing you or a friend who always points out your flaws. You can practice setting limits by politely ending conversations or choosing not to share certain details with someone who only criticizes.
- **Fear of Disappointment**: Some men fear that if they get their hopes up, they will be crushed if things go wrong. In reality, being positive does not guarantee success, but it often improves your chances. Also, positivity can help you handle setbacks with less despair.

3.14 Practical Exercises for Daily Positivity

Below are a few activities that can help you practice positive thinking each day.

1. **Two Good Things**: Each night, write down two good things that happened that day. They can be tiny (like finishing a simple task) or big (like getting a promotion). The goal is to teach your mind to look for what is going right.
2. **Mental Rehearsal**: Before starting your day, close your eyes for a moment and imagine yourself going through your main tasks successfully. You are not lying to yourself about possible challenges; you are simply giving your brain a picture of you handling things well. This can lower anxiety.
3. **Check Your Words**: Pick one day in the week to be very mindful about how you talk about yourself. If you catch yourself using harsh words ("stupid," "hopeless"), replace them with something more fair. This might feel strange at first, but it helps the brain get used to supportive language.
4. **Thank You Notes**: Write a short note or message to someone you appreciate. Expressing gratitude can remind you that life has small positives even during stressful times. It can also improve your relationships.
5. **Pause and Breathe**: When you notice your thoughts becoming hectic, pause. Take a few slow, deep breaths. This short break can help you reset and choose a calmer, more positive angle.

3.15 The Long-Term View

Building positive thinking skills is a long-term process. You might have weeks where your mindset feels strong and you handle stress well. Then a tough situation might happen, and you find yourself falling back into old habits of worry. That is normal. Progress is not always a straight line.

Think of your mind like a muscle that gets stronger with practice. Each time you choose a more supportive thought, you are training that muscle. Over months or years, this can lead to noticeable shifts in how you approach life's ups and downs. You might find that you handle conflict more calmly, recover from setbacks faster, and feel more warmth toward yourself and others.

3.16 Conclusion of Chapter 3

Positive thoughts for daily life do not require you to ignore real problems or pretend everything is perfect. Instead, they involve recognizing negative thoughts when they arise, testing whether they are fair, and then, if needed, adjusting them into something that helps you rather than harms you. By practicing mindful awareness, journaling, and small daily exercises, you can grow a more balanced viewpoint.

This chapter also highlighted that being positive is not about wearing a mask. It is about finding a more balanced stance on reality, seeing both the difficulties and the bright spots. In the next chapter, we will talk about building inner strength. This is closely tied to how you think, because a strong mind often comes from a healthy way of seeing the world. You will learn ways to strengthen your inner core so that when life throws challenges at you, you can remain steady and true to yourself.

CHAPTER 4

Building Inner Strength

Introduction

Men often hear that they should be "strong." But what does that truly mean? Some might picture a man who never cries, never doubts, and never feels anxious. Real strength, however, is more subtle than that. It involves being able to handle tough times, make good decisions, and remain steady in the face of stress. This kind of strength is not just about muscles or showing a tough face. It is about a deep-rooted sense of confidence, clarity, and self-trust.

In this chapter, we will explore how men can build that inner core. We will see how self-discipline, strong values, and a solid view of who you are all contribute. We will discuss how mistakes, setbacks, and even failures can strengthen you if you see them in a certain way. By the end of this chapter, you will have tools and methods to grow that hidden fortress inside yourself, so that when life becomes chaotic, you can stand firm without breaking.

4.1 What Inner Strength Means

Inner strength is the capacity to handle problems without falling apart on the inside. It allows a person to stand by their beliefs while still listening to others. It also helps someone keep going even when tasks seem impossible. Another sign of inner strength is the ability to be honest about your weaknesses or fears, rather than pretending they do not exist.

A man with strong inner resolve does not need to shout or threaten people to get respect. Instead, his steadiness and calm approach naturally draw respect. For instance, if a coworker loses their temper, a man with inner strength will not feel the need to match that anger. He can address the situation calmly, set boundaries if needed, and maintain his composure. That is a clear example of strength that comes from within.

4.2 The Role of Self-Discipline

Self-discipline is often linked to willpower. It is the ability to do what needs to be done, even if you do not feel like doing it. Some people imagine self-discipline as a harsh regime, but it can be more balanced. For example, if you want to get fit, you might set a routine to exercise a few times a week. If you truly value your health, you find a way to stick to this schedule, even on days when you feel lazy.

Self-discipline does not mean you can never rest. Rather, it helps you manage your energy and stick to your important plans. This consistency builds inner strength because you learn that you can rely on yourself to follow through. Over time, each small act of self-discipline adds to your confidence.

4.3 How Values Affect Strength

Values act like a map. They show you what matters most to you, whether it is honesty, loyalty, kindness, or personal growth. When your actions align with your values, you build trust in yourself. You begin to see that you are living in a way that matches your beliefs. This feeling of "being true to yourself" is a major pillar of inner strength.

If you are not clear on what your values are, it can be hard to stand firm. You might find yourself swinging from one idea to another, unsure if you are doing the right thing. Taking time to list your values and think about how they fit into your daily life can help you stand solid. For example, if honesty is a big value for you, that means you speak truth even when it is tough or uncomfortable. Doing so often requires courage, which in turn boosts inner strength.

4.4 Steps to Build Self-Trust

It is hard to be strong inside if you do not trust yourself. Self-trust means believing that you are capable of handling tasks, learning new things, and standing up for yourself. If you have struggled with self-trust in the past, here are some steps that may help:

1. **Make small promises to yourself**: Instead of trying to transform your life overnight, focus on a small, doable promise. For instance, promise that

you will read for ten minutes before bed. Then keep that promise. Over time, these small acts convince your mind that you can rely on your own word.
2. **Write down past successes**: Self-doubt often appears when we ignore the good things we have done. Make a list of times you achieved a goal or solved a tough problem. Review this list when you feel uncertain. It reminds you that you have overcome challenges before.
3. **Admit mistakes without shame**: Everyone makes mistakes. Hiding them or denying them breaks trust in yourself because you are living in a false reality. Admitting an error and learning from it can actually build self-trust, because you see that you can handle the truth.
4. **Look for growth, not perfection**: People who seek perfection often feel disappointed in themselves. Switching the focus to growth—getting a bit better each time—helps build a sense of progress and achievement.

4.5 Physical Practices That Help

Men often ignore how much physical health connects to mental well-being. Simple habits like regular exercise, a balanced diet, and enough sleep can lay the foundation for a stronger mindset. When you exercise, your body releases certain chemicals that can boost your mood and help reduce stress. You also prove to yourself that you can set and follow a plan, which strengthens self-discipline.

Physical practices do not need to be extreme. Even a daily walk can help clear your head. Stretching or basic body-weight exercises can improve how you feel. Getting enough rest each night supports a balanced mood. When your body is taken care of, your mind has an easier time staying strong.

4.6 Mental Practices That Help

- **Meditation or Quiet Time**: Setting aside a few minutes to sit quietly can train your mind to manage stress better. You do not have to do anything fancy. Simply sit still, breathe naturally, and let your thoughts pass without trying to hold onto them. This teaches your mind to release tension and fosters a more stable mood.

- **Reading**: Books and articles about topics you are interested in can expand your mind. Learning new ideas can help you feel more capable. You may also pick up tools for dealing with adversity from authors who have faced similar struggles.
- **Journaling**: Writing down your thoughts helps you process feelings that are hard to understand. Journaling also gives you a record of your progress. You can look back at old entries and see how much stronger you have become over time.

4.7 The Effect of Handling Failure

Failure is often seen as something shameful. Yet failure is a normal part of trying new things or striving for improvement. If you never fail, it might mean you are never taking risks or challenging yourself. How you handle failure can shape your inner strength.

If you fail, you have two choices: beat yourself up or learn from what happened. Learning from failure involves asking questions like, "What specifically went wrong, and what can I do better next time?" This approach keeps your mind on progress rather than self-blame. It also helps you realize that a setback does not define your entire worth as a person.

4.8 Tools for Managing Pressures in Life

Life throws a variety of pressures at men: job demands, family duties, financial worries, and unexpected events. Having practical tools can help you deal with these pressures without losing yourself.

- **Time Blocking**: Spend a bit of time each week planning when you will work, rest, and focus on personal needs. Setting a schedule can help you feel more in control.
- **Delegation**: You do not have to do everything alone. If you feel overwhelmed, look for tasks you can share with others, like a coworker or a family member.
- **Stress Outlets**: A healthy outlet might be a sport, a hobby, or even a simple relaxation technique like deep breathing. The goal is to give your mind a break from constant worry.

- **Talk to Someone You Trust**: Sharing your concerns with a good friend, a counselor, or a support group can give you fresh ideas. It can also remind you that you are not alone.

4.9 Setting Boundaries to Protect Strength

Boundaries are rules you make for how people treat you and how much you give of yourself to others. If you let people cross those lines often, it can chip away at your self-respect and sense of safety. For example, if a friend always calls late at night expecting you to talk for hours, you might feel drained but do it anyway to keep him happy. Over time, this can wear you out.

Creating boundaries might mean learning to say "no." It can also mean telling a coworker you do not feel comfortable discussing certain topics. Some people might not like these boundaries because they were used to having a certain level of access to you. But by standing firm, you protect your mental energy. You also reinforce the message to yourself that you are important enough to draw lines when needed.

4.10 Finding Support through Mentors and Friends

Inner strength does not mean going through life on your own. In fact, having people you trust can boost your confidence. A mentor is someone who has experience and can offer advice. This could be an older coworker, a coach, or anyone you admire. By learning from their experiences, you can avoid mistakes and see new paths to growth.

Friends can be just as crucial. A supportive friend can listen without judgment when you are having a tough day. They can remind you of your strengths and hold you responsible if they see you slipping into harmful habits. Make sure you return the favor, because strong friendships are a two-way street. Often, helping someone else through a hard time can help you feel more capable in your own life.

4.11 Real Examples of Inner Strength in Action

1. **Ray's Story**: Ray was always quiet and never stood up for himself. At work, people would sometimes take credit for his ideas. One day, he decided enough was enough. He made a plan to speak up politely during meetings. At first, it was nerve-racking. But each time he did it, he felt a bit more confident. Over time, coworkers started to see him as a serious contributor. Ray's inner strength grew from a small act of self-advocacy.
2. **George's Story**: George faced a bankruptcy in his early thirties. He felt like a failure and was embarrassed to talk about it. Eventually, he attended a support group for small business owners who had gone through tough times. There, he learned that many had recovered and even thrived later. George decided to pick himself up and start again with a smaller, more focused business plan. After a few years, he found success. He credits his inner strength to the lesson he learned: failing once does not mean you will fail forever.

4.12 Avoiding Pitfalls while Building Inner Strength

- **Arrogance**: Sometimes, when men work on being strong, they might swing too far and become arrogant. True strength does not need to show off. It is calm and steady.
- **Ignoring Emotions**: Being strong does not mean blocking your feelings. If you ignore sadness or worry, it might build up and cause bigger problems later. True strength involves noticing these emotions and dealing with them.
- **Perfectionism**: Trying to be perfect can cause stress and frustration. Remember that strength grows from learning and making progress, not from having zero flaws.
- **Going It Alone**: Thinking you must never ask for help is a trap. That is not strength; it is isolation. Strong men know how to seek support when needed.

4.13 A Short Exercise: "Clarity in Values and Action"

Try this exercise if you want to get clearer on how to build your inner core:

1. **List Your Top 5 Values**: Examples could be "loyalty," "honesty," "fairness," "humor," or "personal growth."
2. **Pick One Value and Link It to Action**: If you choose "honesty," ask yourself, "How can I show honesty this week?" Maybe it is having a talk with a friend about a problem you have been avoiding.
3. **Plan a Time to Follow Through**: Write down the day and time you will take that action. This makes it more real in your mind.
4. **Reflect**: After you do it, write a few sentences about how it went. Were you scared, relieved, or proud? Did it reinforce your sense of being true to your values?

Repeating this exercise with different values can give you practice in lining up your behavior with your inner compass. Over time, living by your values builds a sense of deep trust in yourself.

4.14 The Link between Inner Strength and Calm

When you have built a strong core, you tend to be calmer in stressful situations. This is because you trust yourself to handle problems as they arise. You might still feel nervous or worried, but you have enough experience to know that you can figure out solutions. This calmness can help you make better decisions. It can also help you avoid saying or doing things in anger that you would regret later.

Furthermore, inner strength often means you do not depend on everyone's approval. You might appreciate positive feedback, but you do not crumble if someone disapproves of you. You know who you are, and you have a sense of your own worth. This self-assured stance can actually attract respect and trust from other people because they see you are not constantly seeking validation.

4.15 Conclusion of Chapter 4

Building inner strength involves self-discipline, clear values, self-trust, and the ability to learn from failure. It also includes setting boundaries and seeking support. By taking small steps consistently, you can become a man who stands firm in difficult times without shutting down or lashing out at others.

While it may take effort to grow this kind of inner resolve, it can lead to a life that is more balanced and less shaken by life's ups and downs. As you practice being honest with yourself, setting limits, and caring for your body and mind, you will notice changes in how you respond to challenges. Instead of feeling helpless, you may find you have a sense of quiet confidence.

In the next chapters, we will move on to other aspects of self-improvement, such as handling emotional pain (Chapter 5) and discovering personal interests (Chapter 6). Each topic connects back to both self respect and the power of positive thinking, supporting the larger goal of building a stronger, healthier outlook on life.

CHAPTER 5

Steps to Handle Emotional Pain

Introduction

Emotional pain is part of being human. For men, it can be complicated by social norms or the idea that men should not show sadness or worry. Some men feel they have to be tough and keep everything inside. However, holding pain inside does not usually fix the hurt; instead, it can create more tension. This chapter focuses on how men can handle emotional pain in a healthier way.

We will look at what emotional pain is, why it can feel so strong, and how to deal with it. This includes ways to notice it, talk about it, and keep it from growing out of control. By the end, you should have a clearer sense of how to face deep feelings without feeling weak or ashamed.

5.1 Understanding Emotional Pain

Emotional pain can come from many sources: loss of a loved one, heartbreak, a failed plan, or even a hurtful remark. It can also come from events in childhood or from repeated stress at work. Sometimes, the pain is sudden and easy to trace to a cause. Other times, it feels like a dull ache that is always there, even if you cannot pinpoint exactly why.

One key point is that emotional pain is not a sign of weakness. It is a natural response to events that matter to you. When something goes wrong, your mind and heart react. This reaction signals that something important needs attention. While pain is uncomfortable, it can serve as an indicator that you should pause and check what is happening within you.

5.2 Common Myths about Emotional Pain

1. **"Real men do not feel sadness."**
   This is false. All people feel sadness at times. Men who ignore their sadness may end up overwhelmed in the long run. Recognizing sadness is a normal human process.

2. **"Emotional pain means I am broken."**
   Feeling hurt does not mean there is something wrong with you. It just means your mind and body are responding to a tough situation. That does not make you broken.
3. **"If I let myself feel pain, I will lose control."**
   Many men worry that once they let the pain out, it will become unstoppable. In reality, suppressing pain often leads to unexpected outbursts. When you handle pain in a steady, careful way, it is often less intense over time.
4. **"I must be strong for everyone else, so I cannot show pain."**
   Being strong does not mean ignoring your inner struggles. Often, true strength involves being honest about how you feel and dealing with those feelings in a balanced way.

5.3 Recognizing Emotional Pain

Sometimes, men are not sure if they are experiencing emotional pain or just day-to-day stress. Here are a few signs that you might be dealing with deeper pain:

- Feeling numb or flat, as if nothing matters anymore.
- Constant irritation or anger at small things.
- Thinking about the same sad or hurtful event many times a day.
- Changes in eating or sleeping patterns.
- Losing interest in activities that used to bring enjoyment.

If you notice these signs, it may be time to slow down and acknowledge that you are dealing with something deeper than simple stress. Recognizing the pain is often the first step to healing.

5.4 Steps to Address Emotional Pain Directly

1. **Give Yourself Permission**
   Let yourself admit that something hurts. This does not mean you are weak. It means you are allowing yourself to be honest about your own life.

2. **Name the Pain**
   Try to label what you are feeling. Is it grief, regret, or fear? Simply naming it can bring clarity and reduce confusion.
3. **Find a Safe Outlet**
   This can be talking to a trusted friend, writing in a journal, or seeking professional help. You might also choose a physical outlet, like going for a slow, thoughtful walk and letting your mind work through the pain as you move.
4. **Set a Time to Reflect**
   Schedule a few minutes in your day to sit quietly and observe how you feel. When you give yourself a set time, you limit the worry that these feelings will erupt randomly.
5. **Seek Support**
   Even if you think you must handle it alone, consider reaching out to a counselor, support group, or a mentor. Sometimes, talking to someone who is not directly involved can offer a fresh perspective and a sense of relief.

5.5 The Role of Communication

Talking about emotional pain can feel awkward, especially if you have rarely done it before. But communication is an effective way to process difficult feelings. It does not always have to be a deep conversation with tears involved. It can be as simple as telling a close friend, "I have been feeling stressed. I think it is deeper than simple work stress. Can we chat about it?"

If you find it tough to share with a friend or partner, you might consider a mental health professional who can guide you in expressing painful emotions. A counselor will not judge you; their job is to help you make sense of what you feel and find tools to cope.

5.6 The Physical Body's Reaction to Emotional Pain

Emotional pain can cause physical reactions. Your body might tense up, your heart rate might increase, or you could experience headaches. These physical signs are not imaginary. When your mind is under strain, it signals the rest of your body to react.

Learning to calm the body can also help soothe emotional distress. Techniques like slow breathing, gentle stretching, or a warm bath can help the body relax. When the body relaxes, the mind often follows. If you notice your shoulders tightening up, make a conscious effort to relax them. Over time, this can lower stress and make it easier to cope with emotional pain.

5.7 The Power of Allowing Reality

It is natural to want to push away pain. Nobody likes feeling sad or defeated. However, one of the strongest ways to handle emotional pain is to allow that reality for a moment. Instead of fighting it, you acknowledge it. For instance, if you lost a job you loved, it is okay to sit and say, "I feel hurt and worried right now."

This acceptance does not mean you become passive. It means you are facing the truth instead of trying to hide from it. When you allow the reality of the situation, you can start to make plans for how to handle it. You might decide to update your resume or reach out to contacts about new opportunities. By acknowledging the pain, you open the door to solutions.

5.8 The Difference Between Short-Term Pain and Long-Term Suffering

There is a difference between the short-term pain that comes from a specific event (like an argument or a loss) and long-term suffering that never seems to ease. Short-term pain can be intense, but it often becomes more manageable over time if addressed properly. Long-term suffering might mean there are deeper issues at play—such as old trauma, ongoing anxiety, or repeated stressful situations.

If emotional pain is lasting for months and is affecting all parts of your life, it might be wise to seek professional support. A counselor or therapist can help you uncover hidden issues and provide tools to break the cycle. Understanding whether your pain is short-term or long-term can guide you in finding the right approach.

5.9 Setting Emotional Boundaries

When men are dealing with emotional pain, they may still have to interact with family, coworkers, or friends who need their time. While it is good to help others, setting emotional boundaries can protect you from overextending yourself. For example, if you are grieving a personal loss, you might not have the energy to solve everyone else's problems right now. It is okay to say, "I am going through a hard time. I might not be able to help with that right now."

Setting boundaries can also mean limiting contact with people who trigger negative feelings. This does not mean shutting them out forever. It just means giving yourself space to heal. If a certain conversation topic always makes you feel worse, you can politely say you do not want to discuss it at the moment.

5.10 Real-Life Example of Overcoming Emotional Pain

Victor's Story: Victor was a 35-year-old man who lost a close friend in an accident. He felt so shocked and sad that he avoided talking about it for months. Instead, he threw himself into work and stayed out late with friends. But the heaviness did not go away. One night, he felt a huge wave of sadness and realized he could not keep ignoring it.

Victor talked to another mutual friend of the one who had passed away. They shared memories and both cried. At first, Victor felt weak for crying, but as the conversation ended, he felt a sense of relief. He began seeing a therapist, who taught him ways to handle grief. Through that process, Victor learned that his pain was a normal response to a painful event. Over time, he found healthy ways to remember his friend without feeling consumed by sadness.

5.11 The Role of Self-Kindness

Self-kindness means treating yourself with the same patience and sympathy you would give to someone you care about. When men feel emotional pain, they might also judge themselves for it. They might say, "I should be over this already," or "I am being too emotional." This harsh view can compound the pain, making it even harder to recover.

Instead, self-kindness involves speaking to yourself in a gentle way. You could say, "I am going through a tough time, and it is okay to feel this way for now." Acknowledging your pain without judging it can help the healing process move more smoothly.

5.12 The Problem with Numbing Strategies

Some men turn to strategies to numb their emotional pain. This could be drinking alcohol, using drugs, constantly staying busy, or any behavior that distracts from feeling. While these strategies might provide temporary relief, they usually create larger problems down the road. The pain does not truly go away; it just gets pushed aside.

If you notice yourself reaching for these numbing strategies, try to pause and ask what you really need. Maybe you need a serious talk with someone, or you need rest, or you need a new plan for handling the stressful parts of your life. Replacing numbing tactics with direct steps to handle your emotions can save you from bigger problems in the future.

5.13 Handling Anger in a Healthy Way

Anger can be a mask for deeper sadness or fear. Sometimes, men find it easier to show anger than to show hurt. While anger can be a normal emotion, letting it take over can damage relationships and your own well-being. Handling anger in a healthy way means you notice when it is building up, and you pause before it explodes.

One technique is to step away briefly if possible. You can tell someone, "I need a minute to cool down." Take some slow, deep breaths. If writing helps, jot down why you are angry. This can help you see if there is a deeper cause, like a sense of betrayal or feeling out of control. Once you understand the root, you can talk it through calmly or find another constructive way to handle the situation.

5.14 Helpful Exercises for Emotional Release

1. **Writing a Letter**: Write a letter to the person or situation causing you pain, but do not send it. Just pouring out your feelings can bring relief.
2. **Breathing Practice**: Sit quietly and breathe in for a count of four, hold for a count of four, and breathe out for a count of four. Repeat this cycle ten times. This calms the body and mind.
3. **Physical Movement**: Activities like jogging, swimming, or even brisk walking can help process emotional energy. Movement often helps the mind settle.
4. **Relaxation Audio**: Many short audio recordings guide you through relaxing your muscles and focusing on calm thoughts. Try listening to one before bed or during a lunch break.
5. **Art or Creative Expression**: You do not have to be a skilled artist. Simply doodling or coloring can help express feelings that are hard to put into words.

5.15 Finding a Deeper Meaning

When a painful event happens, some people discover a deeper sense of purpose by reflecting on what they can learn. For instance, if you lose a job, the pain might guide you to rethink your career goals. Maybe you realize you wanted a different path all along. Or if you have a conflict with a friend, you might learn something about the type of people you want close to you.

This does not mean you are glad the painful event happened. It just means you are using it to gain insight. Over time, this new understanding can transform the pain into something that pushes you toward growth. Again, this is not about pretending the pain is good; it is about finding a healthy way to respond that respects your feelings and also leads you to a better outcome in the future.

5.16 Knowing When to Seek Professional Help

If emotional pain lingers for months and affects your sleep, work, or relationships in a major way, it may be time to seek professional help. Signs include thoughts of harming yourself or others, severe hopelessness, or an inability to perform daily tasks. Therapists and counselors are trained to help people move through deep emotional pain. Talking to a mental health professional does not mean you are weak or flawed. It means you care enough about your well-being to get the proper help.

5.17 How to Support a Friend in Emotional Pain

Sometimes, you might be the person someone else turns to. If a friend confides in you that they are hurting, remember a few points:

- **Listen Without Judgment**: Let them speak without jumping in to give advice right away.
- **Ask Clarifying Questions**: If they mention they are sad, ask what might be triggering that sadness. This shows you care.
- **Encourage Them to Seek Help if Needed**: If their situation seems beyond what you can handle, gently suggest they talk to a counselor.
- **Set Your Own Limits**: If their pain is overwhelming for you, it is okay to let them know. You can still be there for them, but you might need to protect your own emotional health.

5.18 Moving Forward Without Guilt

Men sometimes feel guilty after they start feeling better, as if they are betraying the past hurt or the person involved in the pain. It is important to remember that healing does not mean forgetting or dismissing what happened. It just means you are allowing yourself to recover and live fully again.

For example, if you lost someone you love, letting yourself enjoy life at some point in the future does not mean you do not care about that person. It just means you are carrying their memory in a healthier way. Guilt can become another heavy burden if not addressed, so remind yourself that it is okay to heal.

5.19 Long-Term Maintenance

Handling emotional pain is not always a one-time event. Even after you have worked through a tough episode, memories or triggers can pop up later. This is normal. Think of emotional health as an ongoing process. You can keep practicing self-care, communication, and boundary-setting to maintain your well-being.

For instance, you might decide to keep journaling once a week, even when you are feeling good. Or you might continue meeting with a counselor monthly just to check in. Regular maintenance can help you catch any new problems early, before they become overwhelming.

5.20 Conclusion of Chapter 5

Emotional pain does not make you weak or unmanly. It is a normal signal that something needs attention. By learning to recognize pain, speaking about it in a healthy way, and finding proper outlets, men can ease the load of tough emotions. Simple actions like naming your feelings, setting aside time to reflect, and seeking help when needed can shorten the healing process and reduce the damage that ignored pain can cause.

Treating yourself with kindness, acknowledging your limits, and allowing the reality of the situation are key steps. While it can be uncomfortable to face raw emotions, doing so in a steady way often leads to a sense of relief and growth. In the next chapter, we will look at "Discovering Personal Interests"—a topic that, in its own way, can also support your emotional health by bringing new joy and a sense of identity into your life.

CHAPTER 6

Discovering Personal Interests

Introduction
Many men find themselves stuck in routines: go to work, pay bills, take care of basic chores, and repeat. Over time, this cycle can make life feel bland. One reason is that they have not explored personal interests that spark excitement or satisfaction. Personal interests are activities or topics that energize you, whether it is learning a new skill, creating something with your hands, or simply playing a casual sport. In this chapter, we will talk about how to find and develop these interests. We will look at why hobbies and passions matter, how to pick them, and how to stick with them long enough to enjoy real benefits.

Some men believe that finding a personal interest is "not practical" or "a luxury." However, having an activity that matters to you can improve mental well-being, reduce stress, and even open new doors in life. This chapter will show you that discovering personal interests is not just for fun—it is part of a healthy life where you allow yourself to do more than just work and fulfill obligations.

6.1 Why Personal Interests Are Important

Men who do not have outlets for self-expression can become bored or frustrated. Hobbies or interests serve as a way to explore what life has to offer beyond basic chores. They can also help you form new friendships. For example, if you join a local group of people who share your interest, you can build social connections.

Another benefit is that personal interests can help you understand your own talents. You might discover a knack for cooking, drawing, or repairing cars. Even if it never becomes a career, the sense of competence and pride can boost your self-respect. Personal interests also provide a break for your mind from daily stress. They give you something to look forward to, which can prevent burnout in other areas of life.

6.2 Common Barriers to Finding Personal Interests

1. **Lack of Time**
   Many men say they are too busy with work or family. While time is limited, even short sessions (like 15 or 30 minutes) can be used to explore something new.
2. **Fear of Failure**
   Some men worry that they will not be good at the new activity. But part of discovering an interest is the learning process. You do not have to excel immediately.
3. **Financial Concerns**
   Some hobbies can be expensive, but there are also many low-cost or free interests. For example, reading, hiking in nature, or learning a free online skill costs little to no money.
4. **No Clue Where to Start**
   It is common to feel stuck if you have never tried certain activities. That is why we will cover methods to brainstorm and explore possibilities.

6.3 Brainstorming Techniques

If you are unsure what you might enjoy, try a brainstorming exercise. Take a piece of paper and list anything that sparks a bit of interest. Do not judge whether it is practical or if you are good at it. Just write. Could be painting, cycling, bird watching, coding, writing short stories, trying new recipes, etc. Once you have a list, pick one or two that stand out the most and research ways to start.

Another approach is to think about your childhood. Were there any activities you loved but stopped doing as you got older? For example, maybe you used to like building model airplanes or playing a certain sport in high school. Revisiting these old interests can be a good path to finding satisfaction again.

6.4 Past Experiences and Clues

Look back on your life and recall moments when you felt excited or deeply focused on something (even if it was fleeting). Maybe you got really absorbed in a science project or found joy in playing the guitar at a friend's house. These small clues can guide you. They are hints about activities that engage your mind and might offer a sense of personal enjoyment if you were to try them again.

It can also help to talk to people who know you well. Sometimes friends or family have seen sides of you that you overlook. They might say, "You used to light up when you talked about classic cars," or "You are always talking about different movie directors." These observations can point you to areas worth exploring.

6.5 Trying New Things without Pressure

Starting a new activity can be intimidating if you expect instant success. Instead, begin with a beginner's mindset. Tell yourself it is okay to be a novice. Everyone starts somewhere. If you try an art class, do not worry if your first drawings look rough. If you pick up a new sport, expect that you might fumble the ball or miss shots at first.

When you remove the pressure to be perfect, you open the door to growth and enjoyment. You will be able to see if you actually like the activity, rather than judging your enjoyment solely on how skilled you are at it from day one.

6.6 The Role of Mindset

If you go into a new hobby thinking, "I must be great at this right away," you set yourself up for stress. On the other hand, if you approach it with a relaxed mindset, you are more likely to enjoy the learning process. Remind yourself that personal interests are meant to be refreshing. They do not have to produce money or impress others. Their main purpose is to add another layer of happiness or intrigue to your life.

You might also find that a positive attitude can carry over into other areas of your life. For example, if you learn to be patient with yourself while practicing the guitar, you may become more patient at work when learning a new software program. A flexible mindset in one area often leads to improvements in other areas.

6.7 Social Hobbies vs. Solo Hobbies

Some interests work well in groups, like team sports or cooking classes. Others can be solo, like writing or painting. Neither type is better than the other; it depends on your personality and what you need at the time. If you work alone all day, you might enjoy a group hobby to interact with others. If your job is socially demanding, a solo hobby might be more relaxing.

You can also combine both. For example, if you like photography, you can practice alone when you want quiet, or you can join a local photography club for social meetups and photo walks. Mixing these approaches can help you get the benefits of both solitude and connection.

6.8 Budget and Resources

Some men think personal interests are always expensive, but that is not true. Yes, some hobbies—like deep-sea fishing or collecting rare items—may cost a lot of money. However, many interests are budget-friendly. Libraries offer free books and sometimes classes. Many museums have free admission days. Public parks often host free events or let you explore nature at no cost. Online tutorials can teach you a wide range of skills for free, from playing guitar to coding.

Before dismissing a hobby as too expensive, look for low-cost ways to explore it. If you are curious about golf but do not have the funds to play at a fancy course, consider a cheaper local course or a driving range. If you want to try cooking, you do not need the most expensive cookware; basic items can be enough to start learning.

6.9 Overcoming Fear of Looking Foolish

One reason men avoid trying new interests is the fear of looking silly. Perhaps you worry about being the oldest guy at a dance class or the least skilled player on the basketball court. The truth is, most people are focused on their own growth and are not judging you as harshly as you might imagine. Also, many beginners are in the same boat.

If you keep holding back out of fear, you might miss out on something that could bring great joy. The best way to overcome this fear is to take a small step. Sign up for a beginner's class. If it helps, bring a friend. Once you realize that nobody is ridiculing you, the fear often shrinks.

6.10 A Real-Life Example

Darren's Story: Darren was 40 years old and felt stuck in his daily routine. He worked an office job and came home feeling tired. One day, he saw an ad for a local community band. He remembered playing the trumpet in high school but had stopped after graduation. The thought of playing again felt strange. Still, he decided to attend a rehearsal just to watch.

At first, he worried he would be the only older person who was not very good. But he found other adults who were also returning to music after years away. They welcomed him warmly. Darren practiced at home, sometimes making plenty of squeaks and mistakes, but he noticed how satisfying it felt to play again. Within a few months, he was performing in small community shows. It gave him a sense of excitement and a break from his usual day-to-day life.

6.11 Merging Interests with Work

Sometimes, men discover a personal interest that aligns with their career. For instance, a man who enjoys tinkering with software on the side might use that skill to propose a new project at work. Or someone who learns a second language as a hobby might open doors to international travel or new roles in their company. While not every interest has to become part of your job, this possibility shows how hobbies can complement your professional life.

If you are self-employed or run a small business, your personal interests can also inform your brand or products. For example, if you love photography, you might add high-quality images to your business website, making it stand out. The key is to see how the skills or knowledge you gain from your hobby might enhance your professional world, if that feels right to you.

6.12 Activities to Explore Your Likes and Dislikes

Here are some simple exercises to help you figure out what you might enjoy:

1. **Free Choice Day**: Dedicate one weekend day or an afternoon to freely explore. Go to a part of town you rarely visit, step into shops or museums that catch your eye, or try a random class. Write down what you find interesting.
2. **Club Visits**: Check local community boards or online lists for clubs that meet around various topics—board games, gardening, writing groups, etc. Sit in on a meeting. You do not have to commit permanently, but you might discover something new.
3. **Online Tutorials**: Pick a subject you have some curiosity about—like basic coding, sketching, or learning a musical instrument. Watch a free tutorial for 20 minutes and practice for another 20 minutes. See if it intrigues you enough to continue.

6.13 Tracking Your Progress

When you start a new interest, it can be helpful to track your progress in a notebook or an app. This might include:

- Dates and times you practiced or engaged in the activity.
- Small wins or achievements (like finishing your first painting or playing your first song start-to-finish).
- Notes on what you found enjoyable or challenging.

Tracking progress serves two purposes. First, it shows you that you are growing, even if the steps are small. Second, it keeps you motivated because you can look back and see how far you have come. This can be especially important if you hit a plateau or feel tempted to quit.

6.14 Dealing with Setbacks

Every interest has its setbacks. You might hit a point where you do not see much improvement, or you might get too busy for a few weeks and lose momentum. These setbacks are normal. The key is to return to the activity rather than letting it drop completely. Accept that life will sometimes get in the way, but that does not mean your interest has to end.

It might help to reduce the intensity of your practice during busy times. Instead of an hour a day, maybe do 15 minutes every other day until your schedule relaxes. The important thing is to keep a small connection rather than shutting down completely.

6.15 The Link to Self-Esteem

Personal interests can boost self-esteem in several ways. First, you see your skills grow over time, which gives you a sense of achievement. Second, you might receive positive feedback from others who see your work or join you in the activity. Third, you discover that you have the ability to learn new things, which can spill over into other parts of your life.

Men who have at least one interest that they truly enjoy often feel better about themselves. This does not mean you have to become the best at that interest. Just having something that you look forward to can make a big difference in your outlook. It can remind you that life is not just about obligations, but also about personal growth and satisfaction.

6.16 Balancing Interests with Responsibilities

It is important to note that personal interests should not consume your entire life at the expense of work or family duties. The idea is balance. You might schedule a bit of hobby time before work or during a lunch break. Or you might set aside an hour on weekends. Communicate with your family or partner about your interest so they understand why it matters to you.

If finances are tight, pick an interest that does not require big expenses. If your schedule is packed, find something you can do in small pockets of time. The point is to give yourself permission to have an interest while still meeting your responsibilities.

6.17 Expanding Your Comfort Zone

Engaging in new interests can also expand your comfort zone. As you gain confidence in one area, you might be more willing to try other new things. This mindset of exploration can add a sense of excitement to your life. You may discover hidden talents or unexpected passions. Even if you try something and decide it is not for you, you have learned more about your preferences.

This willingness to explore can also show friends and family a different side of you. They might see you as more open or adventurous, which could lead them to invite you to join other activities. Sometimes, one new interest can spark a chain reaction, leading you to experiences you never thought you would have.

6.18 When an Interest Grows into a Passion

Sometimes, what starts as a small hobby grows into a major passion. You may find yourself looking forward to it with excitement each day. For some men, this passion becomes a side business or a new career path. For others, it remains a fun, engaging hobby that balances their regular job.

If you feel that excitement building, consider investing a bit more time or money into it. Take a course, buy better tools, or find a mentor. This does not mean you are obligated to make it your career. Just realize that passions can be a significant source of happiness, so it may be worth giving them more attention if you can.

6.19 Accepting Changes in Your Interests Over Time

It is normal for interests to shift over years. What you love at age 25 might not be the same as what you enjoy at age 45. Life experiences change you, and your hobbies can change too. If you lose interest in something, that is not necessarily failure; it might just mean you have grown or moved on. It can be helpful to revisit your lists or try new brainstorming sessions if you feel your current hobbies are no longer satisfying.

6.20 Conclusion of Chapter 6

Discovering personal interests is not just a pastime—it is a way to add color and excitement to your life. Activities that spark joy or curiosity can also boost your mental and emotional well-being, create social connections, and give you a sense of purpose outside your usual responsibilities. By brainstorming, recalling past experiences, and giving yourself room to learn at your own pace, you can find or revive interests that fit your unique personality.

The key is to approach new hobbies with a spirit of exploration. You do not need to be perfect. You just need to be open to trying and see where that leads. Over time, these personal interests can feed into a stronger sense of who you are, helping you feel more fulfilled in your day-to-day life. In upcoming chapters, we will continue exploring different parts of men's well-being and personal growth, including building a healthy lifestyle (Chapter 7) and forming true friendships (Chapter 8). Each piece builds on the overall aim of helping men stand strong and feel satisfied with who they are.

CHAPTER 7

Tactics for a Healthy Lifestyle

Introduction
Maintaining a healthy lifestyle can feel like a complicated task, especially when life is full of demands from work, family, and daily responsibilities. Yet caring for one's physical and mental well-being is an important part of living well. When men overlook key factors such as good nutrition, regular activity, and proper rest, problems can build up over time. Fatigue can become normal, energy levels can drop, and the risk of illnesses can increase.

This chapter will focus on practical, step-by-step tips to help men shape and maintain a healthy way of living. We will look at the basics of nutrition, how to plan simple exercise routines, the role of rest, and other helpful habits. We will also talk about strategies for stress control and point out how your home or work environment affects your health. By the end, you should feel confident in knowing how to fit healthy practices into your busy schedule.

7.1 What "Healthy Lifestyle" Means

A healthy lifestyle includes choices that support both physical health and mental balance. It is not about being a bodybuilder or eating only greens. Instead, it involves finding a balanced way to nourish your body, stay active, manage stress, and protect your emotional state. For example, a man who works out daily but never allows himself to rest might look fit but feel mentally worn out. A healthy lifestyle ties different elements together so that you feel good physically and mentally over the long haul.

Another important point is that a healthy lifestyle must be practical for you. If you try to adopt routines that do not fit your life, you might drop them quickly. Look for habits that match your schedule, budget, and personal interests. Some men enjoy running, others prefer walking or a team sport. Some like cooking fresh meals at home, others might meal-prep on weekends. The key is finding something realistic so that you can keep it up over time.

7.2 Basic Guidelines for Good Nutrition

Nutrition is a core part of health. The foods you eat affect how you feel, how your body performs, and even how you sleep. But many men feel confused by conflicting advice about diets and foods. Here are some simple guidelines:

1. **Eat a Mix of Nutrient-Rich Foods**
   This includes fruits, vegetables, whole grains, lean proteins (like fish, chicken, beans, or lean cuts of beef), and healthy fats (such as those from nuts, avocados, or olive oil). The idea is to cover different food groups so your body gets a variety of nutrients.
2. **Watch the Portion Sizes**
   Even healthy foods can lead to weight gain if eaten in very large amounts. You do not have to count every calorie, but pay attention to whether you truly feel full. If you do, stop. Keeping portion sizes reasonable helps manage body weight.
3. **Limit Processed Foods and Added Sugar**
   Processed foods can be high in salt, sugar, and unhealthy fats. Soft drinks and sugary snacks can cause energy spikes and crashes, leaving you tired and craving more. Reducing these items in your daily meals can keep your energy more stable and can lower the risk of certain health problems.
4. **Stay Hydrated**
   Drinking enough water is a simple habit that has a big effect on the body. Water helps with digestion, carries nutrients around your body, and keeps your brain clear. Aim for a fair amount throughout the day, and consider using a refillable bottle to remind yourself.
5. **Be Mindful with Alcohol**
   An occasional beer or glass of wine might not cause severe harm, but high or frequent alcohol use can be tough on your liver, stomach, and overall health. Keeping track of your intake and knowing when to stop is an important part of a balanced lifestyle.

7.3 Planning Simple Exercise Routines

Regular activity supports the heart, muscles, and even the mind. It is also a big help in managing weight. Not everyone likes going to the gym, but there are many ways to be active:

1. **Walking**
   A daily walk is an easy and low-cost way to stay active. You can walk during breaks at work, around your neighborhood in the morning, or with a friend in the evening.
2. **Home Workouts**
   If you prefer not to go to a fitness center, do bodyweight exercises at home. Movements such as push-ups, squats, and planks can keep your muscles strong. There are many free videos or mobile apps that guide you step by step.
3. **Sports**
   Joining a local group for soccer, basketball, or another team sport can make exercise fun. It also helps you meet new people. Some men find it easier to stay motivated if they can see activity as a game rather than a chore.
4. **Gym or Group Classes**
   If you like the environment of a gym, that can be a good choice. Group classes—like indoor cycling or martial arts—can also add variety. The key is to pick something that does not feel like a drag so you will keep at it.

Tip: If you are not sure how to start, pick an activity that feels the easiest for you. Maybe it is a 10-minute walk or a quick set of push-ups. Once you get used to it, you can slowly increase the time or intensity.

7.4 The Role of Rest and Sleep

Modern life often encourages pushing ourselves to the limit. Many men feel they have to work late, wake up early, and handle every task without pause. This leads to burnout and poor health over time. Rest is not a waste of time; it is necessary for the body to recharge.

Sleep: Adults generally need about 7 to 8 hours per night, but the exact amount can vary from person to person. Lack of sleep can result in trouble focusing, mood swings, and higher stress levels. It can also contribute to weight gain and lowered immunity. Make sleep a priority by creating a bedtime routine—turning off screens, dimming lights, and winding down in the last hour before bed.

Short Breaks: During the day, small breaks can refresh the mind. Even a quick 5-minute stretch or a short walk can reduce muscle tension and give your brain a breather. If you work at a computer, look away from the screen for a moment or shift your focus to something else to reduce eye strain.

Leisure Time: Setting aside some leisure time to do something you enjoy—like reading, listening to music, or relaxing with a hobby—can help manage stress. It is fine to be productive, but the human body and mind are not built to be in constant work mode without occasional downtime.

7.5 Handling Stress in Daily Life

Stress can show up in many forms: deadlines at work, arguments with a partner, financial worries, or feeling overloaded by demands. If left unchecked, stress can harm your mental and physical health. Here are some methods to handle stress before it grows:

1. **Identify the Source**
   Sometimes, just naming the main stress factor can help you see it more clearly. Is it a particular project at work? A family issue? Once you know, you can figure out what steps to take.
2. **Set Boundaries**
   If you are always saying yes to extra tasks, you might end up overloaded. Try to be realistic about how much you can handle, and learn to say no when you need to. This protects you from taking on too much.
3. **Use Relaxation Methods**
   Deep breathing, quick stretching, or simple meditation can calm the mind. When you feel stress rising, pause for a minute or two and focus on steady, slow breaths. This can lower tension and bring clarity.
4. **Talk It Out**
   Sharing your concerns with a trusted friend, family member, or a counselor can help you find solutions. Sometimes just hearing your own words out loud helps you see what you need to do.
5. **Plan Ahead**
   If your stress is related to being unprepared, try making to-do lists or using a calendar to plan tasks. Breaking big tasks into smaller steps can make them feel more doable.

7.6 Building Healthy Connections with Food and Activity

A healthy lifestyle is not just about forcing yourself to eat "clean" or sweat for hours. It is about finding a balanced relationship with food and exercise. If you see healthy meals as something you "have" to do without choice, you might grow resentful and give up easily. Likewise, if your workout routine feels like punishment, you may lose motivation.

Instead, look for ways to enjoy these habits. Maybe you learn simple, tasty recipes that still include vegetables and lean proteins. Or you join a sports group where you can laugh and compete in a friendly way. The more you see healthy choices as a positive part of your day, the more likely you are to stick with them over time.

7.7 Environment's Effect on Health

Sometimes we forget that our surroundings have a big impact on our lifestyle. If your kitchen is always stocked with junk food, it is harder to stick to healthy eating. If your living space is cluttered, it can add to stress levels. Consider the following:

- **Home Setup**: Keep healthy snacks in easy reach, like fruits or nuts on the counter. Store junk food out of sight or do not buy it in large quantities. Also, make your home environment tidy enough so you do not feel mentally crowded.
- **Work Setting**: If possible, keep a water bottle at your desk and stand up every hour for a short break. See if you can position your computer screen to reduce eye strain. If there is a lot of noise, noise-cancelling headphones might help you concentrate.
- **Commute**: If you drive, can you park farther away so you walk a bit more? If you take public transport, maybe get off one stop early to add some steps to your day. These small changes can add up to a healthier routine.

7.8 Tips for Meal Planning on a Busy Schedule

Time is a big obstacle for many men who want to eat well. Meal planning can help:

1. **Plan Your Meals for the Week**
   Write down what you want to eat for a few days. This stops you from grabbing junk food last minute.
2. **Cook in Batches**
   Cook a big pot of soup, stew, or a dish you like. Store portions in the fridge or freezer. This way you have ready meals throughout the week.
3. **Use Grocery Lists**
   Make a list before you shop so you do not wander the aisles or buy random snacks. Sticking to the list can also save money.
4. **Choose Simple Recipes**
   You do not have to be a master chef. A healthy meal could be grilled chicken with vegetables, whole-grain rice, and a small side of fruit. Many websites or apps offer quick recipes that you can prepare in 30 minutes or less.
5. **Prep Ingredients Early**
   Wash and chop vegetables in advance. Marinate meats the night before. When it is time to cook, the process is faster.

7.9 Keeping Track of Progress without Obsession

It can be helpful to keep track of certain markers like body weight, waist measurement, or the time it takes you to run a mile. This allows you to see if your lifestyle changes are working. However, avoid becoming too fixated on numbers. Health includes more than just the scale. Improvements in energy, mood, and sleep quality are also signs that you are on the right track.

If you see no change after a few weeks, you can adjust your plan—maybe adding a bit more activity or tweaking your meals. Also, be patient. Real changes in health come over months, not days. Quick fixes often do not last, and they can cause disappointment if they fail.

7.10 Staying Motivated Long-Term

The biggest challenge is often sticking to healthy habits. Here are some pointers:

- **Set Realistic Goals**: Instead of aiming for something extreme like losing 20 pounds in a month, aim for a slow and steady improvement.

- **Reward Yourself**: If you hit a milestone, do something enjoyable (not necessarily food-related, like buying a book or going on a fun outing).
- **Find a Partner**: Whether it is a friend who goes to the gym with you or a coworker who shares healthy lunch ideas, having someone on the same path can keep you accountable.
- **Remember Your Why**: Maybe you want more energy to play with your kids or to reduce health risks that run in your family. Keep that motivation in mind when you feel tempted to quit.

7.11 Balancing Work and Health

Modern jobs often involve long hours at a desk. Here are some ways to balance work with physical well-being:

1. **Use Breaks Wisely**: Instead of scrolling on your phone during every break, stand up and do a quick stretch.
2. **Pack a Lunch**: Bringing your own healthy meal can save you from relying on fast food or vending machines.
3. **Short Walking Meetings**: If it fits your workplace culture, suggest a walking meeting for quick discussions. This helps you get up and move.
4. **Watch Your Posture**: Adjust your chair and screen height so you do not slouch. Long-term slouching can lead to back and neck pain.

7.12 Practical Tools and Resources

- **Apps**: Many free apps track your steps, water intake, or calories. While not mandatory, these can offer a sense of accountability if you like data.
- **Online Communities**: There are forums or social media groups where people share meal plans, exercise tips, or motivational posts. Be cautious of misinformation, but these communities can help you stay inspired.
- **Medical Checkups**: An annual physical exam can catch health issues early. It is also a chance to ask your doctor about any concerns you have with your body or mind.

7.13 Real-Life Example: Omar's Shift to Healthier Habits

Omar was a 38-year-old accountant who often felt worn out. He worked long hours, ate fast food during breaks, and rarely exercised. He began to notice his energy levels dropping and his waistband getting tighter. A routine doctor visit showed high blood pressure and a warning that he might develop certain health problems if he kept his current habits.

Omar decided to start small. He replaced sugary drinks with water and cut down on takeout meals. He also started walking for 20 minutes each night, just around his neighborhood. After a few weeks, he noticed a slight boost in energy and saw that he was saving money by not ordering food all the time. Motivated, he added simple home workouts and began experimenting with easy, healthy recipes. Over the span of a year, Omar lost weight, reduced his blood pressure, and felt more alert each day. He also found that his mood improved when he was less stressed about his health.

7.14 Avoiding Extreme Diets and Exercise Plans

It is tempting to try extreme solutions that promise quick fixes, like very low-calorie diets or intense workout programs that push you to the limit. These approaches might give fast results in the short term, but they are often hard to keep up and can cause harm to your body or mind. Balance is key. A moderate diet that includes a variety of foods is usually healthier than a fad diet that removes entire food groups. Likewise, a reasonable exercise plan you can stick with is better than an extreme workout that makes you quit after a week.

7.15 The Role of Mental Health in a Healthy Lifestyle

Physical and mental well-being are closely connected. If you are stressed, anxious, or dealing with emotional struggles, it can be tougher to eat properly or follow an exercise schedule. You might feel drained or lack motivation. That is why it is important to be mindful of your mental state, too. Seek help if you notice ongoing low mood, worry, or trouble coping with daily life. A balanced lifestyle includes acknowledging emotional needs as well as physical ones.

7.16 Setting Yourself Up for Success

Below are some suggestions to help you transition to healthier habits in a steady way:

1. **Start with One Habit at a Time**
   Trying to change every habit at once can be overwhelming. Focus on one area, such as drinking more water or adding a 15-minute walk, then build from there.
2. **Use Reminders**
   Put a note on your fridge to grab a fruit instead of a candy bar, or set an alarm on your phone to stand up and stretch if you sit for long periods.
3. **Make It Convenient**
   If you want to exercise in the morning, place your workout clothes and shoes next to your bed. If healthy snacks are accessible, you are more likely to choose them.
4. **Learn About Health**
   Read books, watch documentaries, or follow reliable health experts online. Understanding the "why" behind good nutrition and exercise can increase your motivation.
5. **Track Your Mood and Energy**
   Keep a small log of how you feel on days you stick to your plan. Over time, you might see a link between healthy habits and improved energy or better focus.

7.17 Social Support for a Healthy Lifestyle

Changing your way of living can be easier if people around you support your efforts. If your household members are on board, you can plan meals together or encourage each other to work out. If your friends see you making healthier choices, they might be curious and join in. You can also find local meetup groups that organize runs, hiking trips, or other activities. Being part of a supportive network helps you stay motivated and feel less alone in your goals.

7.18 Overcoming Setbacks

It is normal to slip up occasionally. You might have a busy week and grab fast food multiple times or skip several workouts. Instead of giving up, see it as a bump in the road. Get back on track as soon as you can. Remind yourself that building a healthy lifestyle is a long-term process, not a short race. Even small improvements can add up significantly over a year or more.

7.19 Adapting to Different Life Stages

Your health needs can change as you age or as life circumstances shift. A new job might alter your schedule, or an injury might limit your usual exercise options. Adapt your routines in a way that respects these changes. You might try a gentler form of exercise or adjust your meal patterns if your work hours shift. The main idea is flexibility—letting your lifestyle evolve to fit your current situation while still keeping health as a priority.

7.20 Conclusion of Chapter 7

A healthy lifestyle comes from consistent, balanced habits in nutrition, movement, rest, and stress control. You do not need to be extreme or perfect. Instead, focus on steady changes that match your life. Whether it is a 10-minute walk, a few minutes of stretching, or a decision to pick water over soda, every small choice can make a difference over time.

The benefits of these tactics extend beyond the physical. When you feel better in your body, you often feel more confident and less weighed down by stress. This chapter offered guidelines on how to shape a healthy way of living, from meal planning to handling stress. As we move forward, we will look at how friendships and connections also play a key role in overall well-being. Taking care of your body and mind prepares you to connect with others in a stronger, more positive manner.

CHAPTER 8

True Friendships and Connection

Introduction
Healthy friendships and genuine connections with others give life more depth. Men, in particular, may find it challenging to form or maintain close bonds because of social expectations or a worry about appearing weak. Some men stick to surface-level conversations, discussing sports or work, but not opening up about deeper subjects. Over time, this can lead to feelings of isolation or a sense that something is missing.

In this chapter, we will look at what true friendship means and how men can build connections that are honest and supportive. We will discuss how to form new bonds, strengthen existing ones, and even spot relationships that may be harmful. By practicing certain skills and being open to deeper conversation, men can experience a sense of belonging and companionship that is vital for emotional wellness.

8.1 Why Real Friendships Matter

Humans are social beings by nature. Even the most independent man needs some level of connection. True friends can offer support during difficult times, share good memories, and challenge you to become a better person. They can also be a source of honest feedback when you need it, or a source of laughter when you are feeling low.

Loneliness can lead to stress, depression, and a range of physical health problems. On the other hand, having friends who truly care about you can reduce stress levels and create a support system. Genuine connections can also make life more fun and meaningful, whether you are gathering for a social event, playing a casual sport, or simply talking one-on-one.

8.2 Foundations of Healthy Friendships

- **Trust**: Without trust, a friendship stays on the surface. Trust means you feel safe sharing thoughts and experiences because you believe your friend will respect your privacy.

- **Mutual Respect**: In a real friendship, both parties value each other's opinions and personal space. You might not always agree, but you show understanding for each other's viewpoints.
- **Honesty**: Hiding behind lies or half-truths weakens any bond. Being honest, even when it is uncomfortable, helps a friendship grow.
- **Support**: A good friend is someone who roots for your success, comforts you in loss, and is willing to offer help or listen when you need it.

When these elements are present, a friendship can flourish. If you sense that one of these pieces is missing, it might be a sign the relationship needs attention.

8.3 How to Start New Connections

Building friendships does not need to be forced or awkward. Still, many men feel unsure about how to meet new people as adults. Here are some suggestions:

1. **Join Activities or Clubs**
   Look at local community centers, sports leagues, or hobby groups. When you share an activity, the conversation flows more naturally because you already share a common interest.
2. **Attend Events**
   Workshops, local gatherings, or volunteer events can be a good place to meet like-minded individuals. When you attend something that truly interests you, you have an immediate topic to chat about.
3. **Leverage Current Contacts**
   Sometimes, a friend of a friend might become a close connection if you share common ground. Do not be afraid to accept invitations or reach out to acquaintances.
4. **Online Platforms**
   There are online groups where people discuss shared hobbies or local events. While online connections might not always lead to real friendships, they can be a starting point.

Note: Taking the first step might feel awkward at times, but many adults are also looking for new friends. Taking a small risk and saying hello can open the door to a new connection.

8.4 From Small Talk to Deeper Conversations

Many men stay in the zone of small talk about weather, sports, or work routines. While small talk is fine for casual chats, deeper friendships often form when people share personal experiences or feelings. Here are tips to transition from surface-level topics to more meaningful conversation:

1. **Ask Open-Ended Questions**
   Instead of "Did you have a good weekend?" try "What was the most interesting thing you did this weekend?" This invites more detail.
2. **Share a Bit About Yourself**
   True conversation is a two-way street. Reveal something about your own life—an opinion, a memory, or a funny story. This can encourage the other person to do the same.
3. **Listen Actively**
   Pay attention, ask follow-up questions, and show that you genuinely want to understand. Avoid jumping in with your own story too quickly. This approach makes the speaker feel valued.
4. **Be Patient**
   Not every chat will go deep right away. Give it time. As trust grows, conversations often become more personal.

8.5 Maintaining Existing Friendships

Friendships can fade if not nurtured. Work, family, and life changes can make it hard to stay in touch. Here are ways to keep friendships strong:

1. **Regular Check-Ins**
   This can be a quick message, call, or plan to meet for coffee. Even short connections show you care.
2. **Shared Experiences**
   Plan activities you both enjoy—watching a sports match, going for a hike, cooking a meal together. Shared experiences create new memories and reinforce the bond.
3. **Honest Communication**
   If something is bothering you, do not let it build up. Politely bring it up before it sours the relationship. Likewise, if your friend brings up an issue, listen calmly.

4. **Celebrate Milestones**
   Birthdays, promotions, or personal achievements are chances to show support. A simple text or small gathering can strengthen the bond and show you appreciate them.

8.6 The Concept of Emotional Closeness

Emotional closeness means feeling comfortable enough to share personal thoughts or feelings without fear of harsh judgment. This does not require constant deep talks, but it does involve being able to trust each other on a personal level. Men who allow themselves to open up often discover a sense of relief and a richer friendship. They realize they do not have to face challenges alone.

Not every friend will become this kind of confidant, and that is okay. Some friendships remain at a moderate level of closeness, focused on shared interests. But having at least one or two close friends can be a big boost to mental health. It offers a place to discuss worries, celebrate good news, and simply be yourself.

8.7 Identifying Warning Signs in Friendships

Not all relationships are supportive. Sometimes, men stay in friendships that drain them or harm their self-esteem. Watch out for these red flags:

- **Lack of Respect**: If a friend constantly mocks you or puts you down, it may be more than just harmless teasing.
- **One-Sided Effort**: If you are always the one calling or making plans, and the other person rarely reciprocates, you might be carrying the entire friendship by yourself.
- **Unhealthy Influence**: If a friend repeatedly pushes you to do things that go against your well-being—like heavy substance use or risky behavior—you may need distance.
- **No Real Support**: If they never show up when you truly need help or always brush off your problems, the relationship might be superficial.

It can be hard to realize that a friendship is unhealthy, but letting go or reducing contact with negative influences can free up space in your life for more uplifting connections.

8.8 Conflict Resolution with Friends

Conflict is natural in any close relationship. Differences in opinion or misunderstandings can arise. The key is resolving these issues in a respectful way:

1. **Stay Calm**
   When upset, it is easy to snap. Take a moment to breathe before responding.
2. **Use "I" Statements**
   Instead of saying "You always do this," say, "I feel hurt when this happens." This approach focuses on feelings rather than pointing blame.
3. **Listen**
   Give your friend a chance to explain their view. Sometimes, conflicts happen because of simple misunderstandings.
4. **Seek Common Ground**
   Look for areas where you both agree. Then, figure out what steps you can take to move forward.
5. **Agree to Disagree if Needed**
   Some issues might never be fully solved, and that is okay. As long as you respect each other's different viewpoints, you can continue the friendship.

8.9 How Social Circles Change Over Time

It is normal for social circles to shift as you enter different stages of life—college, marriage, fatherhood, job changes, etc. Some friends may naturally drift away if your interests or living situations no longer match. This does not always mean a failed friendship; it can just mean the nature of the connection changes.

If you lose touch with someone you value, you can try reaching out again. A simple message can sometimes rekindle a friendship. Other times, it might become clear that you have both grown in different directions. Accepting that change can be a healthy part of moving forward.

8.10 Balancing Alone Time and Social Time

Some men are more introverted and need extra alone time to recharge. Others thrive on being around people. There is no one-size-fits-all rule about how much social interaction you need. The important thing is to find a balance. If you lean heavily on alone time, try to schedule at least some social events or calls to maintain those bonds. If you are very social, remember to allow friends space as well. Healthy friendships respect each person's comfort level.

8.11 Friends in Different Circles

You might have work friends, gym friends, old childhood friends, and neighbors. Each group can play a unique role in your life. Some may share professional goals, others might share personal hobbies. Embrace the variety. You do not have to merge them all into one big group. Having friends in different circles can expand your perspectives and experiences.

For example, your work friends might understand job-related stress better, while your gym friends might motivate you to stay active. A childhood friend might know your family history and be someone you can speak to about personal topics. You can benefit from each friendship in its own way, without feeling pressured to make everyone meet each other.

8.12 Online Friendships and Social Media

In the digital age, online friendships are more common. You might chat with someone you met through a game, a forum, or social networks. These bonds can be real and meaningful, but be aware of potential pitfalls. Sometimes, people present themselves differently online. Also, time spent on social media can become addictive, pulling you away from real-life interactions.

If you form a strong online bond, treat it with the same values of trust, honesty, and respect as you would an offline friendship. But also try to balance screen time with face-to-face contact. Digital communication is a tool, not a total replacement for in-person connection.

8.13 Handling Rejection and Friendship Breakdowns

Not everyone will want to be your friend, and some friendships might end. This can be painful, but it is part of life. If someone turns down your invitation or stops contacting you, do not take it as a personal flaw. People have different schedules, interests, or issues in their lives that might prevent them from bonding with you at that moment.

If a close friendship ends after a disagreement or hurtful event, it is normal to feel upset. You can try to patch things up with honest talks, but sometimes both parties choose to walk away. In such cases, focus on lessons learned. Did you discover something about communication, respect, or boundaries that you can use in the future?

8.14 The Role of Humor and Fun

Laughter can form a bond that goes beyond words. Friends who share a sense of humor often find relief during stressful times by joking around. Fun activities—like playing a game, watching a comedy, or going to an amusement park—can bring people closer. Humor should never be used as a mask to hide serious problems, but it can be a healthy way to lighten the mood and keep a friendship enjoyable.

8.15 Supporting Friends Through Tough Times

Being a good friend does not just mean having fun together. It also means standing by someone when life gets rough. If your friend is dealing with loss, health issues, or job stress, here are some guidelines:

- **Listen Fully**: Let them vent without rushing to fix the situation.

- **Offer Practical Help**: This could be driving them somewhere, helping with tasks, or simply checking in.
- **Respect Their Space**: Some people want to talk right away, others need time alone before opening up.
- **Encourage Professional Help if Needed**: If their problems seem serious—like signs of deep sadness or harmful thoughts—gently suggest they speak with a mental health professional.

You might not have all the answers, but your presence can be comforting. This support often strengthens the friendship further because it shows genuine care.

8.16 When Friends Grow Apart

It can be sad to feel a close friend slipping away. Maybe one person moved to a new city, or schedules clash, or interests have changed drastically. Acknowledging that the bond may not remain the same is part of respecting each other's lives. You can try setting a routine call or occasional visits if distance is the issue.

Still, if attempts to stay connected do not work and one person stops responding, it might be time to let it rest. Recognize the good memories you shared and be open to reconnecting later if the situation changes. People change with time, and friendships sometimes shift as well.

8.17 Group vs. One-on-One Dynamics

Some friendships form in a larger group. Group settings can be lively and offer multiple connections at once. However, you might find that smaller gatherings or one-on-one meetups allow more depth in conversations. Balancing both types of social interactions can give you the benefits of wider social fun and deeper personal talks. If you only see friends in group events, you might not get many chances to have meaningful conversation. Scheduling a coffee or dinner with just one friend can open the door to more honest communication.

8.18 Bringing Vulnerability into Male Friendships

Men are often told to be strong or not show too much emotion. This can lead to friendships that never touch on real feelings or problems. However, allowing a bit of vulnerability can actually bring men closer. For example, expressing that you have been stressed about work or that you feel uncertain about a major decision can encourage your friend to share, too. This mutual openness builds a different level of trust.

You do not have to share every detail of your life to be authentic, but acknowledging that you have emotions and concerns shows you respect yourself and your friend. Over time, such openness can lead to more stable and loyal friendships.

8.19 The Positive Impact on Overall Well-Being

Strong friendships can contribute to better mental and physical health. Spending time with others can reduce loneliness and improve mood. Good friends also hold you accountable, whether it is encouraging you to keep healthy habits or reminding you to stay true to your values. Studies have shown that people with supportive social networks often cope better with stress and may even have a lower risk of certain health problems.

Combining a healthy lifestyle (as discussed in Chapter 7) with strong social ties can create a strong foundation for overall wellness. When you take care of your body and keep meaningful connections, you are more likely to feel balanced and less likely to slip into unhealthy patterns.

8.20 Conclusion of Chapter 8

Real friendships and honest connections are not just extras in life—they play a key role in a man's mental and emotional health. By understanding the basics of trust, respect, and supportive communication, men can form connections that go beyond small talk. These bonds serve as a source of joy, support, and personal growth. Whether you are forming new friendships through shared hobbies or strengthening ties with lifelong friends, the principles remain the same: honesty, respect, and mutual care.

Allowing yourself to be open in your friendships does not reduce your masculinity. It can, in fact, help you stand stronger in tough times. If you recognize signs of a negative or one-sided connection, it is okay to step away or set boundaries. The goal is to surround yourself with people who respect you, challenge you in a positive way, and share genuine moments of understanding and fun.

In the next two chapters, we will move forward to explore building a productive mindset (Chapter 9) and learning good communication skills (Chapter 10) in more detail. These topics connect with friendships and healthy living by showing you how to approach tasks and interact with others in a balanced, effective manner. As you keep reading, you will see how each element ties into becoming the best version of yourself.

CHAPTER 9

Building a Productive Mindset

Introduction

A productive mindset is more than just completing tasks. It involves how you structure your time, the way you approach problems, and the attitudes you maintain when facing challenges. Some men think being productive means never resting or working long hours without pause. But true productivity arises from steady effort, clear planning, and wise use of resources—including your own mental and physical energy.

This chapter will lay out ways to build a mindset that supports consistent output without causing you to burn out. We will look at setting practical goals, managing distractions, and creating a plan that fits your own life situation. By using these ideas, men can get more done in less time while keeping a balanced outlook. Whether you are a full-time worker, a parent juggling many duties, or someone hoping to use free time better, the strategies in this chapter can support you.

9.1 Understanding a Productive Mindset

At its core, a productive mindset is about viewing tasks and challenges with clarity. Rather than feeling constantly rushed or overwhelmed, you focus on steady progress. This approach also includes self-awareness. For example, you know when you work best (morning, afternoon, or night) and arrange your most demanding tasks during that window. You recognize your limits and avoid planning too many tasks at once.

A productive mindset does not mean you will never have lazy moments or times when you are stuck. It means that you have habits that help you bounce back. When you lose focus, you have methods to regain it. When a project is too big, you have ways to break it down. This chapter will dig into specific tactics and tips to help you build those habits.

9.2 The Role of Clear Goals

Working without clear goals is like driving without a destination. You might travel, but you may not go anywhere useful. Goals guide your actions, giving you a target to aim for. When you have a well-defined goal, you can plan the steps needed, measure your progress, and see which parts need more attention.

1. **Set Specific Goals**
   Vague goals such as "I want to do better at work" do not give you a map. Change it to something more concrete, like "I want to complete my project proposal by next Friday." Now you have a deadline and a clear outcome.
2. **Make Goals Realistic**
   If you set goals that are impossible to reach—like finishing a three-month project in a week—you set yourself up for failure. Realistic goals consider the time, resources, and support you have.
3. **Break Down Big Goals**
   Large goals can be scary. If you want to get in shape, that might feel too broad. So break it down: maybe aim to run twice a week for 20 minutes or plan a simple workout routine for 15 minutes a day. These smaller tasks are easier to start and less overwhelming.
4. **Use Timelines**
   Having a timeline helps you see how your goal fits into your week or month. It can be as simple as writing tasks on a calendar. Timelines also allow you to track your pace and make changes if you fall behind.

9.3 Overcoming Procrastination

Procrastination is the habit of pushing tasks to the last minute, often because we feel the task is boring, scary, or too difficult. It can lead to rushing, mistakes, and extra stress. Overcoming procrastination does not require superhuman willpower; it involves understanding why you delay and making small changes.

1. **Identify the Reason**
   Is the task too unclear? Are you anxious about failing? Or is it just not interesting? Pinpointing the reason can help you address the core issue. If the task is unclear, break it into smaller, clearer steps. If it feels scary, remind yourself that small progress is better than doing nothing.

2. **Use the "Five-Minute Start"**
   This technique involves telling yourself you will work on a task for just five minutes. Often, once you start, you realize it is not as bad as you feared and keep going. The hardest part of many tasks is just beginning.
3. **Set Early Deadlines**
   If you know you tend to wait until the last minute, plan your own deadline earlier than the actual one. For instance, if your boss needs a report by Friday, aim to complete it by Wednesday. This buffer can reduce stress and give you time to fix mistakes.
4. **Reward Yourself**
   Once you finish a task you were dreading, treat yourself. This could be as small as taking a short break, listening to your favorite music, or enjoying a nice meal. Over time, your brain starts to link completion of tasks with something positive.

9.4 Time Blocking and Scheduling

Time blocking is a method where you divide your day into blocks, each dedicated to a certain task or type of activity. This can prevent you from hopping between tasks and losing focus. For example, you might block off 9:00 a.m. to 10:00 a.m. for replying to emails, 10:00 a.m. to 12:00 p.m. for working on a report, then 1:00 p.m. to 2:00 p.m. for errands. During each block, you concentrate fully on the assigned task.

- **Why It Works**: The human mind does better with focused time on one project rather than constant switching. Multitasking seems useful, but often lowers efficiency.
- **How to Use It**: Begin by listing your main tasks for the day. Estimate how much time each task will need, and then place them into your schedule. Include short breaks so you do not burn out.
- **Sticking to Blocks**: Turn off unnecessary notifications and close unrelated browser tabs during each block. If a new task appears, jot it down to handle later, rather than dropping everything to do it now.

9.5 The Power of Routines

Routines reduce the mental load of decision-making. When you have a set routine—like a fixed morning schedule—you do not have to waste mental energy thinking, "What do I do first?" You simply follow the plan. This can make your day run more smoothly.

- **Morning Routine**: Many people find that how they start the day sets the tone. A morning routine might include waking up at a certain time, stretching or doing a quick workout, having a simple breakfast, and reviewing the day's tasks.
- **Evening Routine**: This could involve tidying your workspace, making a list of tasks for tomorrow, and winding down with something relaxing—like gentle reading or calming music.
- **Adjust Over Time**: If a routine feels stale or is not helping, adjust it. The goal is to create a flow that reduces stress, not to lock yourself into a rigid plan that no longer suits your life.

9.6 Handling Distractions

Distractions can wreck productivity. Whether it is social media, constant notifications, or chatty coworkers, these interruptions break your focus. Regaining that focus can be tough, leading to a chain of unproductive moments. Here are ways to handle distractions:

1. **Mute or Turn Off Alerts**
   If possible, silence non-essential notifications on your phone or computer. You can check messages at set times rather than every time you hear a beep.
2. **Create a Focused Space**
   If your home or office environment is noisy, use noise-canceling headphones or find a quieter spot. Even a simple "Do Not Disturb" sign can help if you share space with others.
3. **Use Website Blockers**
   If you find yourself wandering onto social media or news sites too often, consider using apps or browser extensions that block time-wasting sites for specific periods.
4. **Set Break Times**
   Instead of randomly checking your phone throughout the day, decide that

every hour or two, you will take a short break to check messages or move around. This way, you are in control of when distractions are allowed.

9.7 Dealing with Burnout

Burnout is a state of physical, mental, and emotional exhaustion. It often occurs when someone pushes themselves for too long without proper rest or balance. Men who try to handle a heavy workload or manage family duties and side projects can reach a point where motivation disappears and small tasks feel impossible.

- **Signs of Burnout**: Chronic fatigue, irritability, lack of interest in usual tasks, and feelings of being stuck.
- **How to Recover**: First, recognize that burnout is not a sign of laziness. It is your body and mind signaling that they need rest. Cut back on non-essential tasks, set firmer limits at work, and schedule true downtime. You may also need to speak with a counselor or doctor if burnout is severe.
- **Preventing Burnout**: Build regular rest into your life. This includes daily breaks, weekly relaxation activities, and yearly vacations if possible. Also, learn to delegate tasks when you can. You are not meant to handle everything alone.

9.8 Using Simple Tools for Productivity

You do not need fancy software or complicated systems. Many highly productive people use basic tools like:

1. **To-Do Lists**
   A piece of paper with the day's tasks can be just as effective as a digital app. Cross off tasks as you complete them, which gives a sense of progress.
2. **Calendar**
   Whether it is a physical planner or an online calendar, seeing tasks laid out over days or weeks helps you plan and avoid scheduling conflicts.
3. **Task Managers**
   Apps like Trello, Asana, or a basic reminder app can help you organize

bigger projects into stages. They can be useful if you prefer digital systems, but they are optional.
4. **Timers**
The "Pomodoro" technique involves working in blocks (often 25 minutes) and then taking a short break. Setting a timer helps you stay on track and reminds you to rest.

Remember: the tool you choose matters less than how you use it. If a simple notebook works for you, stick with it.

9.9 Staying Motivated When Results Are Slow

Some goals, like learning a new skill or building a business, do not show big results quickly. This can be discouraging. Here are ways to stay motivated during long projects:

1. **Track Small Wins**
Even if you are far from the final outcome, note down little achievements: completing a chapter of a course, gaining a first client, or improving a skill. These mini-successes remind you that you are moving forward.
2. **Review Progress**
Every week or month, look back at where you started. Compare your current state with your initial state. Often, you will see you have grown more than you realized.
3. **Adjust If Needed**
If you keep hitting barriers, maybe you need a new approach. Talk to someone who has experience in that area or do some research. Changing tactics is not failing; it is part of learning.
4. **Remember Why You Started**
Think about your core reason for the goal. Perhaps you wanted a healthier body, a new career, or more freedom. Keeping that purpose in mind fuels you when you feel frustrated.

9.10 Balancing Work with Personal Life

A productive mindset is not about putting all your energy into work alone. If you ignore personal life and family, you can create tension and burn out sooner.

Balancing does not mean equal time for everything, but it does mean giving space to important areas of your life.

- **Make Personal Activities Non-Negotiable**: If you want to exercise or spend time with family, schedule it as you would an important work meeting. When you treat personal items as optional, they often get canceled first.
- **Set Clear Work Boundaries**: If your job expects you to be reachable 24/7, try to negotiate more reasonable hours. Constant availability can drain mental energy.
- **Plan for Relaxation**: Keep an evening free each week or plan a small weekend outing. This can recharge you and help you return to work more focused.

9.11 Learning from Mistakes

Mistakes are part of the growth process. A productive mindset involves learning from errors rather than ignoring them or letting them destroy your confidence. If you miss a deadline because you planned poorly, identify where you went wrong. Did you underestimate how long the task would take? Did you get distracted? By examining these details, you can improve next time.

Sometimes, men feel shame over mistakes, seeing them as signs they are not good enough. Shifting your perspective can help: a mistake shows you a gap in your plan. Once you fix that gap, you can handle future tasks better. This approach keeps you moving forward rather than stuck in guilt.

9.12 Building Mental Resilience

Resilience is the ability to keep going under stress or when things do not go as planned. It is linked to a productive mindset because it helps you adapt to changes and recover from setbacks.

- **Practice Flexibility**: Life rarely goes exactly as planned. If you are too rigid, any small issue can throw you off. With flexibility, you can shift course without losing your overall sense of direction.

- **Keep a Positive Yet Realistic View**: Try not to interpret every challenge as a disaster. Look for what can be done, even if it is small.
- **Use a Support System**: Friends, mentors, or coworkers can offer fresh ideas and moral support. Talking through issues often reveals solutions you might not see alone.
- **Self-Care**: Exercise, good nutrition, and adequate sleep strengthen both body and mind, making you more resilient to stress.

9.13 Leveraging Mentors and Role Models

Men often benefit from having a mentor or role model who has achieved what they hope to achieve. This does not mean copying every step, but seeing how they structure their day, handle stress, and stay motivated. If you can directly talk to a mentor, ask them how they set goals, what tools they use, and how they overcame major setbacks.

Role models can also be found in books or online talks. Even if you cannot speak to them in person, you can learn from their experiences. Notice that many successful people highlight consistent effort, openness to feedback, and a willingness to keep learning. These qualities are at the heart of a productive mindset.

9.14 Avoiding Common Pitfalls

While building a productive mindset, watch out for these traps:

1. **All-or-Nothing Thinking**
   Believing you must either do something perfectly or not at all can lead to stagnation. It is better to try and achieve 80% of your aim than not to try at all.
2. **Overloading Your Schedule**
   Some men get excited about improving productivity and load up on tasks. Soon, they are overwhelmed again. Instead, start with small changes. Once those become routine, add more if you have capacity.
3. **Comparing Yourself to Others**
   Seeing someone else's success can be motivating, but it can also lead to

envy or panic if you feel you are not matching their pace. Everyone has different strengths and backgrounds. Focus on your own path.

4. **Never Taking a Break**
   Working nonstop might look impressive at first, but it can hurt your performance in the long run. Breaks give your mind a chance to recharge and can actually improve creativity.

9.15 Real-Life Example: Marcus's Shift in Mindset

Marcus worked as a sales manager and often felt like he was juggling too many tasks. He would start projects but never finish them on time, and he ended most days feeling drained. After a talk with a more experienced colleague, Marcus realized his lack of structure was the problem.

He decided to try time blocking. Every evening, he wrote down the three most important tasks for the next day. Then he divided his schedule into focused blocks for each task. He turned off his phone alerts during these blocks and only checked emails during two specific times a day. Within a week, he noticed he was completing tasks faster and still had energy left. Marcus also found that seeing tasks neatly laid out reduced his mental clutter.

Over the next few months, Marcus refined his approach, learning to estimate task durations more accurately. He also scheduled short breaks to walk around and clear his mind. His sales performance improved, and his stress levels dropped. Marcus realized that a productive mindset did not mean working non-stop. It meant working smarter with a plan he could actually follow.

9.16 Sustaining Momentum

Building a productive mindset is not a one-time event. It is an ongoing practice. Once you find methods that work—like time blocking, daily to-do lists, or a specific routine—you continue using them. If life circumstances change, you adjust. For example, a man who becomes a father might need to move some of his focus blocks to earlier mornings or handle tasks in smaller chunks.

Regular self-reflection helps sustain your momentum. Perhaps every Sunday, you look at what went well that week, where you struggled, and how you can improve. Over time, these small tweaks add up to big gains in productivity and balance.

9.17 Using Stress for Positive Drive

While too much stress is harmful, a small amount can inspire you to act. Some men find they work best when they set slight challenges for themselves—like aiming to finish a task an hour earlier than usual. This mild pressure can sharpen focus. The trick is to keep stress at a moderate level. If stress becomes overwhelming or constant, it turns into a barrier rather than a motivator.

9.18 Emotional Factors in Productivity

Productivity is not just a mechanical system of tasks and schedules. Emotions play a huge role. If you are feeling sad, anxious, or resentful, it can be hard to focus or stay motivated. Paying attention to your emotional state helps you catch signs that something is off. You might need a day of rest, a talk with a friend, or a short break to handle personal issues. A productive mindset respects the fact that humans have emotions, and ignoring them can harm overall performance.

9.19 The Bigger Picture: Purpose and Values

Some men discover they are most productive when their tasks align with a bigger sense of purpose or personal values. For instance, if you value helping others, you might feel more driven working on community projects or roles that let you serve clients directly. If creativity matters to you, tasks that involve designing, writing, or problem-solving might spark more enthusiasm.

When you align daily actions with what you care about, you often gain a deeper motivation that keeps you going even when tasks become difficult. Taking time to figure out your personal values can guide the choices you make about work, hobbies, or volunteer projects.

9.20 Conclusion of Chapter 9

Building a productive mindset requires setting clear goals, structuring your time effectively, and handling obstacles like procrastination and distractions. It also means keeping a healthy balance so that you do not burn out or lose sight of important personal values. This approach is sustainable because it respects both your ambitions and your limits.

While it may take time to shift from feeling scattered to feeling structured, each small change—like creating a consistent morning routine or learning to say "no" to extra tasks—can yield noticeable improvements. The result is more steady progress toward your goals and a daily life that feels manageable rather than chaotic. In the next chapter, we will move from internal organization to outward expression by exploring "Skills for Good Communication." These two subjects go hand in hand because a clear mindset and strong communication often support each other in work, relationships, and personal growth.

CHAPTER 10

Skills for Good Communication

Introduction
Being able to express yourself well is a cornerstone of personal and professional success. For men, communication can be tricky. Some fear appearing too emotional, while others struggle to put thoughts into words. Yet the ability to clearly share feelings, ideas, and needs is vital in all areas of life—work, friendships, romantic relationships, and beyond.

In this chapter, we will look at what good communication involves, including how to listen actively, use body language effectively, and speak honestly yet respectfully. We will also discuss how to tackle conflict in a healthy manner. Whether you want to improve your job performance, have deeper conversations with friends, or handle disagreements at home, these communication skills can help.

10.1 Why Communication Skills Matter

Clear, respectful communication builds trust. It helps avoid misunderstandings that lead to anger or broken relationships. In the workplace, strong communication can make you a better leader or teammate. At home, it fosters closeness and mutual support. Even in everyday life—like dealing with customer service or talking to neighbors—the ability to speak and listen effectively can make interactions smoother.

On the other hand, poor communication can cause confusion, resentment, and lost opportunities. When you do not express your true feelings or needs, others may not know how to respond. When you do not listen properly, you miss important details that could solve a problem or strengthen a bond. Improving communication takes practice, but each step brings noticeable benefits.

10.2 Active Listening

Active listening is more than just hearing the words someone says. It involves fully focusing on the speaker, showing understanding, and responding in a thoughtful way. Here are key elements:

1. **Pay Attention**
   Put aside distractions like your phone. Look at the speaker. Nod or use simple verbal responses like "I see" or "That makes sense" to show you are tuned in.
2. **Do Not Interrupt**
   Wait until the speaker finishes. Cutting them off can send the message that you do not value what they have to say.
3. **Ask Clarifying Questions**
   If something is unclear, ask, "Could you explain a bit more about that?" This shows genuine interest and helps you gather details.
4. **Reflect Back**
   Summarize what you heard in your own words: "So you are saying that you feel unappreciated at work. Did I get that right?" This step ensures you understood correctly and gives them a chance to correct you if needed.

Active listening builds trust because the other person feels heard. It also helps prevent misunderstandings. You might be surprised how much you learn when you really listen rather than waiting for your turn to speak.

10.3 Clarity in Speaking

Men sometimes worry about sharing feelings directly. They might drop hints or use sarcasm instead of stating what they need or feel. Clear speaking means stating your point with honesty and directness, but not in a rude or harsh way.

- **Use "I" Statements**: Instead of blaming with "You never listen," try "I feel ignored when I try to share something and do not get a response." This approach reduces defensiveness.
- **Keep It Simple**: Long-winded explanations can confuse the listener. Try to sum up your main message in straightforward terms: "I need help on this project," or "I am disappointed that our plans changed."
- **Provide Context**: If the topic is complex, give brief background details. Explain why you feel a certain way or what led to your request. Context helps the other person see the bigger picture.
- **Use the Right Tone**: The same words can sound caring or harsh depending on your tone. If you are calm, people are more likely to hear what you are saying rather than focus on how you are saying it.

10.4 Nonverbal Communication

Research shows that a large portion of communication is nonverbal. This includes facial expressions, posture, gestures, and eye contact. Nonverbal cues can strengthen your words or contradict them. For example, if you say "I am glad to see you" while rolling your eyes or looking away, the listener will sense a mismatch.

1. **Eye Contact**
   Looking at the person while talking shows sincerity and interest, but avoid staring too intensely. Aim for a natural level of eye contact.
2. **Facial Expressions**
   Keep your expression in line with your message. If you are discussing something serious, a serious expression can convey empathy.
3. **Posture**
   Slouching or crossing your arms might appear defensive or disinterested. Sit or stand up straight, and face the person you are speaking with.
4. **Hand Gestures**
   Moderate use of gestures can help emphasize points. Waving your arms wildly can distract the listener, while keeping arms locked at your sides can appear stiff or detached.

10.5 Adapting to Different Communication Styles

People have different styles of communication. Some are straightforward and direct, while others are more cautious. Some prefer talking face-to-face, while others do better in writing. Recognizing and adapting to these styles can reduce friction.

For example, if you have a coworker who is more reserved, bombarding them with loud jokes or demanding immediate answers may push them away. Instead, you might give them time to process before they respond. Or if you have a friend who is very direct, do not take it personally if they speak bluntly. Their style might just be more concise. Respecting these differences helps build smoother interactions.

10.6 Handling Conflict in a Healthy Way

Conflict is natural in any relationship. The difference is how you handle it. Here are steps to face conflict without damaging the connection:

1. **Stay Calm**
   Raising your voice or using insults can escalate the situation quickly. If you are angry, take a brief moment to cool down.
2. **State the Issue Clearly**
   Focus on the specific problem, not the person's character. "I felt left out when I was not told about the meeting," is better than "You always forget about me!"
3. **Listen to Their Side**
   Even if you disagree, let them explain. Ask questions to clarify. This shows you value their viewpoint.
4. **Look for Solutions**
   The goal is not to "win" the argument but to solve the issue. Brainstorm options that might work for both parties.
5. **Agree on Next Steps**
   End with a plan or agreement on how to prevent the same conflict in the future. It might be scheduling regular check-ins or promising to speak up earlier when problems arise.

10.7 Empathy in Communication

Empathy means recognizing and understanding someone else's feelings. You do not have to agree with everything they say, but you try to see where they are coming from. This skill can transform the way you talk to others.

- **Put Yourself in Their Position**: Imagine how you would feel if you were in their situation. This can soften your tone and make your words more kind.
- **Use Validating Phrases**: Saying, "I understand why you would feel that way" or "That makes sense to me" shows you hear them.
- **Avoid Dismissing Feelings**: Phrases like "You are overreacting" or "That is silly" shut down the other person. Even if you do not share their feeling, respect that it is real to them.

Empathy can reduce tension and help both sides feel safer opening up.

10.8 Asking Good Questions

Asking questions can keep a conversation going and show that you are genuinely interested. However, the type of questions you ask matters:

1. **Open-Ended Questions**
   These cannot be answered with a simple yes or no. Examples: "What do you think about this approach?" or "How did you get started in that field?" They invite the other person to share more.
2. **Follow-Up Questions**
   If someone mentions an event, ask more about it: "How did you feel about that?" or "What happened next?" This encourages deeper conversation.
3. **Avoid Leading Questions**
   Leading questions push the person to give a specific response. For instance, "You agree that this policy is stupid, right?" is not neutral. If you want an honest answer, ask without bias: "What do you think of this policy?"

10.9 Being Present in Conversations

Being present means you are mentally there, not just physically. If you are daydreaming or thinking about your to-do list, you might miss details. Some tips:

- **Eliminate Distractions**: Put your phone away or silence it. If you are constantly glancing at it, the speaker may feel unimportant.
- **Use Your Body Language**: Lean in slightly when someone speaks. Maintain eye contact. These cues show you are engaged.
- **Practice Mindful Listening**: When you notice your mind drifting, gently bring it back to what the other person is saying.

10.10 Constructive Feedback

Whether at work or in personal relationships, feedback helps people improve. Constructive feedback is different from criticism that tears someone down. It focuses on behavior and outcomes, not personal attacks.

- **Be Specific**: Say what behavior or outcome can change, rather than making broad statements. "You were late to the last two meetings" is more helpful than "You are always irresponsible."

- **Offer Suggestions**: If possible, provide ideas for improvement: "Could you set a reminder or leave earlier to avoid traffic?"
- **Balance Negative with Positive**: Mention what the person did well, too. This shows you see their efforts and strengths.
- **Ask for Their View**: Feedback is a two-way process. Ask how they feel about it or if they have ideas on how to improve.

10.11 Receiving Feedback with an Open Mind

Being on the receiving end of feedback can be uncomfortable. Men sometimes feel the need to defend themselves to preserve pride. However, being open to feedback is a sign of growth and maturity.

- **Listen Fully**: Do not interrupt with excuses. Let the person explain.
- **Ask Clarifying Questions**: If something is unclear, ask for examples.
- **Avoid Taking It Personally**: Focus on the specific behavior or result that needs changing. It does not define your entire worth as a person.
- **Decide What to Do**: You do not have to follow every piece of feedback blindly, but at least consider it. If multiple people point out the same issue, it might be a real area for improvement.

10.12 Communication in Group Settings

Speaking in a group can feel more tense than one-on-one conversation. Good group communication involves balancing speaking time, listening to others, and making sure everyone feels included.

1. **Stay on Topic**
   Group discussions can derail if people go off on tangents. If you see this happening, gently steer the talk back.
2. **Encourage Participation**
   If someone is quiet, invite them to share: "Sam, do you have any thoughts?" This shows you value their input.
3. **Share the Floor**
   Avoid dominating the conversation. Give others space to voice their opinions.

4. **Summarize Key Points**
   After some back-and-forth, it can help to briefly summarize main ideas or decisions. This helps everyone stay on the same page.

10.13 Dealing with Different Opinions

When two people disagree, it does not have to lead to heated arguments or personal insults. Differences can be a chance to learn.

- **Keep It About the Idea**: Focus on the idea itself, not the person.
- **Stay Curious**: Ask why they see it that way. This might reveal new information.
- **Look for Common Ground**: Even if you differ on major points, you might agree on smaller ones. Build from there.
- **Know When to End**: Sometimes, you cannot persuade the other person, and they cannot persuade you. It is all right to end a discussion with a polite statement like, "I see where you are coming from, but it seems we still differ."

10.14 Communication in Romantic Relationships

Strong communication is crucial in romantic partnerships. Small misunderstandings can become big conflicts if not handled early. Here are some guidelines:

- **Check In Regularly**: Ask your partner how they are feeling and if there is anything on their mind.
- **Express Appreciation**: Simple words of gratitude can strengthen the bond.
- **Share Concerns Promptly**: If something bothers you, speak up kindly before it grows into resentment.
- **Learn Their Style**: Some partners need a bit of quiet time to process feelings, while others want to discuss right away. Adapting to each other's style can prevent fights.

10.15 Technology and Communication

In the digital age, texting and social media can make communication easier but also more confusing. Written messages do not carry tone of voice or facial expressions, which can lead to misunderstandings.

- **Read Before You Send**: Check if your words could sound harsh when read quickly.
- **Limit Arguments via Text**: Complex or emotional topics are often best handled by voice call or face-to-face.
- **Be Mindful of Tone**: Use polite language in emails and messages, especially if it is a professional setting.
- **Use Emojis or Punctuation Carefully**: While they can help express tone, going overboard might confuse the other person or come off as unprofessional (in work contexts).

10.16 Dealing with Communication Anxiety

Many men experience anxiety when speaking in public or approaching difficult talks. This can come from fear of judgment, worry about rejection, or lack of practice. Overcoming anxiety involves:

1. **Preparation**: If it is a planned talk or presentation, practice what you will say. This helps you feel more confident.
2. **Breathing Techniques**: Before speaking, take slow, deep breaths. This calms the body.
3. **Positive Self-Talk**: Remind yourself, "I have something worthwhile to say," or "I can handle this."
4. **Gradual Exposure**: Start with smaller groups or simpler conversations. Build up your confidence step by step.

10.17 Humor as a Communication Tool

Appropriate humor can ease tension, make points memorable, and show you are approachable. However, humor can also be risky if it offends someone or distracts from important issues. Use humor carefully:

- **Read the Room**: Make sure the situation is okay for jokes. Serious matters need a respectful tone.
- **Avoid Offensive Jokes**: Humor should not involve mocking someone's background, beliefs, or vulnerabilities.
- **Self-Deprecating Jokes**: A gentle joke about your own minor flaws can show humility, but do not put yourself down too harshly or often.

10.18 Building Long-Term Communication Skills

Like any skill, communication improves with practice and reflection. Consider these steps to keep growing:

1. **Reflect After Interactions**
   Ask yourself what went well and what could have been handled better. This awareness helps you fine-tune your approach.
2. **Seek Constructive Critiques**
   Ask trusted friends or mentors how you come across in conversation. Their insights can reveal blind spots.
3. **Learn from Role Models**
   Observe good communicators around you. Notice their tone, timing, and how they handle interruptions.
4. **Stay Curious**
   Communication evolves with technology and social changes. Keep an open mind and be willing to adapt.

10.19 Real-Life Example: Leo's Workplace Communication

Leo worked in a busy office. He often had good ideas but struggled to express them in meetings. His boss once asked for suggestions, and Leo hesitated, thinking, "Maybe it is not that good." Later, he saw another coworker propose a similar idea, which got positive feedback.

Realizing he was holding himself back, Leo decided to practice speaking up. He started small by sharing brief comments in shorter team huddles. He also worked on being concise. Instead of rambling, he outlined his thoughts on paper before the meeting. As time passed, Leo's coworkers noticed he had valuable input. He became more confident, and his boss invited him to present at a major client meeting. Leo's communication skills not only benefited his career but also helped the team succeed.

10.20 Conclusion of Chapter 10

Good communication is a key skill that affects nearly every aspect of life. From resolving conflicts at work to discussing worries at home, how you speak and how you listen determine whether problems shrink or grow. Using methods like active listening, clear and honest speaking, and empathy can improve relationships and help you feel more understood as well.

Learning to communicate well is an ongoing process. Each conversation gives you a chance to practice patience, understanding, and clarity. As you refine these skills, you may notice that you resolve misunderstandings faster, feel less frustration, and form stronger connections. Moving forward, chapters 11 and 12 will continue to add to this overall toolkit by covering how to handle conflict in various settings (like work and home) and how to manage shame and guilt in a constructive way. By combining good communication skills with an open mindset, you position yourself to face life's ups and downs with more confidence and less regret.

CHAPTER 11

Managing Conflict at Work and Home

Introduction
Conflict is a normal part of human interaction. People have different views, needs, and ways of handling problems. Whether in the workplace or at home, disagreements will arise. The important part is how we address them. Men who develop better conflict management skills often find that their relationships run more smoothly, and they experience fewer unresolved issues.

In this chapter, we will look at strategies to handle arguments or clashes in a constructive manner. We will focus on both professional settings (like dealing with bosses, colleagues, or customers) and personal settings (like talking with family, spouses, or children). By learning these strategies, you can reduce the stress that conflict brings and create an environment where problems are solved in a fair and respectful way.

11.1 Recognizing Conflict Early

Many disagreements start small, perhaps as a minor misunderstanding. If not addressed, the issue can grow until it becomes a bigger problem. Learning to notice early signs—such as irritated tone, avoidance of certain subjects, or sudden changes in behavior—can help you step in before things worsen.

- **Pay Attention to Tone**: If a coworker's or family member's tone shifts suddenly from calm to tense, it might mean a conflict is brewing.
- **Look for Unspoken Signs**: Avoidance, heavy sighs, or closed-off body language can indicate someone is upset even if they do not say it out loud.
- **Ask a Quick Question**: A simple "Hey, everything okay?" can bring small concerns to light, giving you a chance to address them before they escalate.

11.2 Common Sources of Conflict

Understanding common causes can help you see why disagreements happen and how to prevent them:

1. **Differences in Values or Priorities**
   For example, one person might think saving money is top priority, while another believes in spending for comfort.
2. **Poor Communication**
   Misunderstandings often stem from unclear instructions or incomplete information.
3. **Competing Goals**
   At work, two departments may have different objectives that clash. At home, one partner may want to focus on traveling, while the other wants to focus on fixing the house.
4. **Personality Clashes**
   Some people are very direct, others are more sensitive. These traits can cause friction if not understood.
5. **Stress or Exhaustion**
   When people are tired or overwhelmed, even small issues can spark conflict because patience is lower.

By identifying these triggers, you can catch yourself or others before tension grows too large.

11.3 Conflict Styles

Everyone has a style of handling conflict. Some are quick to argue, others withdraw, and some try to smooth things over. Researchers have identified a few main styles:

- **Avoiding**: Steering clear of the conflict altogether, hoping it goes away. Sometimes useful for small, unimportant issues, but dangerous for big problems.
- **Competing**: Insisting on your own way, often at the expense of others. Can be useful in urgent crises but can damage relationships over time.
- **Accommodating**: Yielding to what the other person wants. Helps keep the peace but can lead to feeling taken advantage of.

- **Compromising**: Both sides give up something to reach a middle ground. Better than constant fighting, though each person might feel partially unsatisfied.
- **Collaborating**: Trying to find a solution that meets everyone's needs. Takes time and effort but can lead to better, lasting outcomes.

Men who learn to shift between these styles, depending on the situation, often handle conflict more effectively. However, many conflicts can benefit from collaborating or at least a balanced compromise.

11.4 Steps for Managing Conflict

Here is a basic roadmap you can follow when you sense disagreement escalating:

1. **Stay Calm**
   If you feel your emotions rising, take a short pause. Breathe deeply, count to ten, or politely ask for a moment to gather your thoughts. This keeps anger or frustration from taking over.
2. **Identify the Real Issue**
   Sometimes, people argue about surface topics when the real problem lies deeper. For instance, a heated debate over chores might actually be about feeling unappreciated. Ask yourself or the other person, "What's the main concern here?"
3. **Use Open Communication**
   Each side should explain what they want or need, and why it matters to them. For example: "I need you to share updates on this project so I can plan ahead," or "I need some alone time after work to recharge."
4. **Listen Actively**
   Give the other side space to talk without interrupting. Then paraphrase what they said to ensure you understand correctly.
5. **Look for Options**
   Brainstorm possible solutions. Could tasks be divided differently? Could you schedule a weekly check-in? Generate ideas without immediately judging them.
6. **Reach a Conclusion**
   Agree on a specific plan or compromise. Make sure each person knows their part, how they will carry it out, and by when.

7. **Follow Up**
   After some time, check in to see if the plan is working. If not, adjust it. Recognize successes or improvements to reinforce positive behavior.

11.5 Conflict at Work: Specific Tips

Work conflicts can be especially tense because people's jobs and reputations are at stake. Here are some suggestions:

1. **Focus on Behaviors, Not Personal Traits**
   Instead of accusing someone of being "lazy," refer to missed deadlines or incomplete tasks. Focus on observable actions.
2. **Approach Privately if Possible**
   Do not call people out in front of an entire team unless absolutely necessary. A private conversation often leads to a more open exchange without embarrassment.
3. **Document Facts**
   If the conflict involves performance or a project, keep relevant emails, notes, or data. This keeps the discussion anchored in evidence rather than emotion.
4. **Escalate Wisely**
   If you cannot resolve the issue on your own, bring it to a supervisor or HR. But do so in a calm manner, explaining the situation clearly and providing possible solutions.
5. **Stay Professional**
   Even if the other person is emotional, keep your tone polite. You are there to address a problem, not to tear each other down.

11.6 Conflict at Home: Specific Tips

Conflicts at home often involve strong emotions because family is personal. Whether with a spouse, children, or extended family, the stakes feel higher. Some guidelines:

- **Set a Calm Time to Talk**
  Avoid bringing up issues when you or your partner is in the middle of

something stressful. Pick a time when both can focus without distractions.
- **Use Respectful Language**
  Hurtful remarks can leave lasting scars. Even in heated moments, choose your words carefully.
- **Acknowledge Feelings**
  If your child is upset, for example, say, "I see you are frustrated," or "I understand this is hard for you." This shows them you are not dismissing their emotions.
- **Create House Rules for Disagreements**
  These could include no yelling, no name-calling, and giving each person a chance to speak. When a conflict arises, remind everyone of these rules.
- **Team Approach**
  If you and your partner disagree, try seeing yourselves as a team facing the problem, instead of seeing each other as the enemy. Ask, "How can we solve this together?"

11.7 Dealing with Ongoing Tension

Some conflicts do not go away after a single conversation. There might be repeated disagreements due to major differences in beliefs, values, or personalities. In these cases:

1. **Look for Patterns**
   Do these conflicts happen at a certain time or about a certain topic? Recognizing patterns can help you see solutions.
2. **Consider Outside Help**
   Couples therapy, family counseling, or mediation can guide you through tough, long-running disputes. This is not a sign of weakness; it shows you value the relationship enough to seek professional support.
3. **Try New Approaches**
   If the same argument keeps occurring, the old methods clearly are not working. Maybe try writing down each side's concerns and reviewing them calmly. Or set a weekly "discussion hour" where issues can be raised constructively.
4. **Know Your Limits**
   If the conflict is toxic—such as someone's well-being or safety is at risk—you might have to consider more drastic steps, like ending the

relationship or seeking legal advice. Protecting yourself and loved ones must be a priority.

11.8 Emotional Intelligence in Conflict

Emotional intelligence is the ability to recognize, understand, and manage emotions—both your own and others'. High emotional intelligence helps with conflict because you can stay calm and read the situation better.

- **Self-Awareness**: Know when you are getting heated. Recognize the physical signs, like clenched fists or a racing heart, and take steps to calm down.
- **Empathy**: Imagine how the other person feels. A small sign of understanding can defuse tension.
- **Self-Regulation**: Instead of snapping back, you learn to pause and choose a measured response.
- **Social Skills**: Good communication, active listening, and the ability to navigate disagreements are all part of emotional intelligence.

11.9 Nonverbal Clues

Nonverbal cues—body language, eye contact, tone—play a major role in conflict. You might say the right words, but if your arms are crossed and your expression is angry, the other person might feel threatened.

- **Tone of Voice**: Keep your voice steady and measured. Avoid shouting, whining, or sarcasm.
- **Body Posture**: Facing the person and uncrossing your arms shows openness. Leaning forward slightly can signal engagement, but do not loom over them.
- **Facial Expressions**: Tight jaw, rolling eyes, or a smirk can escalate tension. Stay aware of what your face is conveying.

When you display calm and open body language, the other person is more likely to respond in a similar way.

11.10 Handling Conflict with Children

Children do not have the same emotional control as adults. They can throw tantrums or become defensive quickly. To manage conflict with kids:

1. **Stay Calm**
   Your composure sets the tone. If you yell, they learn that yelling is how to handle disagreements.
2. **Explain Rules and Consequences**
   If there is a conflict about chores, for instance, calmly state what is expected and what will happen if chores are not done. Consistency is key.
3. **Acknowledge Their Feelings**
   Children often just want to know they are heard. Saying, "I see you are upset that you cannot play right now," can help them feel understood.
4. **Offer Choices**
   Giving a child limited options can reduce power struggles. For example, "Do you want to clean your room now, or in 10 minutes?"
5. **Teach Skills**
   Use conflicts as lessons on how to express frustration, take turns, and solve problems. Children learn a lot by watching how adults handle disputes.

11.11 Avoiding "Winner vs. Loser" Thinking

Many men are taught to compete, to be the "winner." In conflict, this mindset can be harmful. If you treat every disagreement as a battle to be won, the other person becomes the "loser." This approach might bring short-term victory, but it can damage trust and closeness over time. Instead, think about how both sides can benefit from a fair solution or compromise.

11.12 Conflict When You Are the Boss

If you manage people at work, you must address conflicts among your team. Leaving them to "work it out themselves" can lead to bigger issues that affect morale and productivity.

- **Set Clear Expectations**: Make sure everyone understands their roles, goals, and deadlines. Many workplace conflicts come from confusion about responsibilities.
- **Be Fair and Consistent**: If you handle one person's lateness strictly but ignore another's, conflict and resentment can grow. Apply rules consistently.
- **Give Constructive Feedback**: When you see tension building, talk to the involved parties privately and suggest ways to resolve it.
- **Promote a Culture of Respect**: Reward teamwork, good communication, and constructive problem-solving. Call out disrespectful behavior early.

11.13 Conflict with Difficult Personalities

Some individuals seem to create conflict wherever they go. They might be overly critical, controlling, or quick to anger. While you cannot change someone's personality, you can alter your reactions.

- **Set Boundaries**: Politely but firmly let them know what behaviors are not okay with you. If they continue, limit your interaction if possible.
- **Stay Objective**: Try not to take their comments personally. Difficult people often act out due to their own issues, not because of you.
- **Choose Your Battles**: Decide whether the issue is worth addressing. If it is minor and will not affect your well-being or work, you can opt to let it go. If it is major, approach the conflict with a calm plan.
- **Seek Support**: If dealing with a truly toxic person (like a bullying coworker or an abusive family member), talk to HR, a counselor, or someone else who can guide you in next steps.

11.14 Repairing Relationships After Conflict

Sometimes, harsh words or strong emotions can damage trust. Repairing that bond requires effort:

1. **Apologize Sincerely**
   If you are at fault, a direct apology without making excuses can go a long way. For example, "I realize I spoke unfairly. I am sorry for my tone. I want to fix this."

2. **Allow Time for Healing**
   The other person may need time to process feelings. Pushing them to "get over it" quickly can backfire.
3. **Change the Behavior**
   An apology is less meaningful if the same behavior continues. Show with actions that you are committed to better handling of conflict next time.
4. **Show Positive Effort**
   A small gesture—like a note or a kind act—can signal that you genuinely want to move past the argument.
5. **Learn from the Conflict**
   Think about what sparked it and how you both can avoid repeating the same pattern.

11.15 Using Humor Wisely

Humor can sometimes defuse tension—if used well. A light, gentle joke can help people see the conflict is not a do-or-die situation. But be careful:

- **Do Not Mock**: If someone is upset, a joke at their expense can make them feel belittled.
- **Check the Tone**: Some conflicts are too serious for humor. If someone feels deeply hurt, they may see humor as you not taking them seriously.
- **Use Self-Directed Humor**: If anything, joke about your own small slip-ups or misunderstandings, not the other person's. This can show humility.

11.16 When to Agree to Disagree

Some conflicts do not have a neat solution. It might be about politics, personal preferences, or beliefs that neither side will change. Sometimes, the best route is to respect each other's viewpoint without trying to "win."

- **Set Boundaries on the Topic**: If the issue triggers fights every time, agree not to talk about it, or agree to limit conversations to specific times.
- **Find Shared Interests**: You might still connect over hobbies, sports, or shared experiences, even if you do not share certain beliefs.
- **Accept Imperfection**: We cannot see eye-to-eye with everyone on every subject. That is part of life.

11.17 Stress Control During Conflicts

It is normal to feel anxiety or anger during disputes. Managing this stress is crucial for staying rational:

- **Breathing Techniques**: Slow, deep breaths calm the fight-or-flight response.
- **Physical Outlet**: If possible, take a walk or move around briefly. This can burn off nervous energy.
- **Focus on Solutions**: Direct your mind to practical steps rather than fueling the anger.
- **Positive Internal Talk**: Remind yourself you can handle this. Simple thoughts like, "I can stay calm" or "This will pass" can keep you centered.

11.18 The Role of Empathy in Conflict Resolution

Empathy can shift the tone of a conflict from adversarial to collaborative. By understanding the other person's concerns, you can often find compromises more easily.

- **Listen for What Is Unsaid**: Sometimes, people speak in angry tones when they really feel hurt or scared.
- **Show You Care**: Even if you disagree, say, "I see this is really important to you."
- **Ask About Their Interests**: Ask gentle questions to learn more about why they need something. This might reveal new ways to solve the problem.

11.19 Conflict Prevention

While not all disputes can be stopped beforehand, many can be minimized through proactive actions:

- **Clear Expectations**: In the workplace, set clear goals and responsibilities. At home, discuss roles and schedules.
- **Frequent Communication**: Regular check-ins can catch small issues before they become big ones.

- **Mutual Respect**: Treating others with kindness, even when stressed, fosters an environment where conflicts are less likely to erupt.
- **Personal Well-Being**: When you are well-rested and managing your stress, you are less likely to snap or overreact.

11.20 Conclusion of Chapter 11

Conflict management is a skill that can reduce stress and protect relationships. By recognizing early signs of tension, choosing respectful communication, and aiming for problem-solving rather than "winning," you can handle disagreements in a healthier way. These principles apply equally to work settings and to the home, though the methods may vary in detail depending on the environment and the people involved.

Healthy conflict resolution does not mean you will never argue. It means you have constructive ways to address issues, keep respect intact, and emerge with solutions or at least understanding. The next chapter (Chapter 12) will look at a different but related area of emotional health: managing shame and guilt. These feelings often arise when conflict has led to regrettable words or actions, or when men blame themselves for not meeting expectations. By learning to face shame and guilt properly, you can strengthen your emotional stability and continue growing as a person.

CHAPTER 12

Overcoming Shame and Guilt

Introduction

Shame and guilt are heavy feelings that can weigh on a man's sense of worth. They often arise after conflict, mistakes, or failures, but they can also come from deeper, long-standing issues—like childhood experiences or cultural pressures. Shame and guilt can shape how we view ourselves. They can also cause us to pull away from friends, family, or goals.

This chapter explores what shame and guilt really are, how they differ, and how to address them in a constructive way. We will look at signs that these emotions have taken over and steps men can take to break free from negative thought patterns. By facing these emotions directly, it is possible to reduce their power and build a healthier self-image. This process might feel uncomfortable at first, but it leads to a more balanced way of living.

12.1 Defining Shame and Guilt

While people often use these terms together, they have slightly different meanings:

- **Guilt**: Feeling bad about something you did or failed to do. It is usually linked to a specific action or inaction. For instance, you might feel guilty for lying to a friend.
- **Shame**: Feeling bad about who you are as a person. This is deeper and less tied to a single event. Someone who feels shame may think, "I am worthless" or "I am fundamentally flawed."

Guilt can lead to positive changes if handled properly—like apologizing or fixing a mistake. Shame, however, can be harder to address because it affects your entire sense of self.

12.2 Common Causes of Shame and Guilt

1. **Mistakes and Failures**
   A major project at work failing, being fired from a job, or letting family members down can lead to guilt or shame.
2. **Past Experiences**
   Childhood criticism, bullying, or being told you are not good enough can cause deep shame that lasts into adulthood.
3. **Society and Culture**
   Sometimes, men feel guilty or ashamed if they do not meet certain standards of strength, success, or stoicism.
4. **Relationships**
   Hurtful words from a partner or friend can make a person question their own worth.
5. **Personal Expectations**
   If your inner standards are extremely high, you might feel guilt or shame whenever you fall short, even if your slip-up is minor.

12.3 Signs That Shame or Guilt Are Controlling You

It is normal to feel guilt or shame occasionally, but when these emotions become too strong, they can disrupt your life. Signs include:

- Constant self-criticism or negative self-talk.
- Avoiding social events because you feel unworthy or embarrassed.
- Persistent feeling that you "do not deserve" happiness or success.
- Anger or irritability stemming from suppressed guilt.
- Overcompensating, such as always trying to prove your worth to others.

If these signs appear regularly, it might be a clue that shame or guilt has taken an unhealthy hold.

12.4 The Difference between Healthy and Unhealthy Guilt

Healthy Guilt:

- Connected to a clear behavior that went against your values.

- Encourages you to make amends or change.
- Fades once you have corrected the situation or learned from it.

Unhealthy Guilt:

- Hangs around even after you have apologized or tried to fix the mistake.
- Is not tied to a specific wrongdoing but more to a sense of being "bad."
- Leads to self-punishing thoughts or actions that do not resolve the core feelings.

Knowing which type you are experiencing can guide you in how to respond.

12.5 The Role of Childhood Messages

Often, shame grows when someone has been repeatedly told, "You are bad," instead of "Your action was bad." Children absorb these messages deeply. Over time, they may come to believe they are flawed at their core.

For instance, if a boy grows up hearing phrases like, "What is wrong with you?" or "You never do anything right," he may internalize shame. As an adult, he might fear taking on new challenges or blame himself for events outside his control.

Recognizing these old messages is the first step to breaking their hold. It might help to write down what you remember being told and ask yourself if those words were fair or just someone else's negative way of speaking.

12.6 Rewriting Your Inner Script

Shame often lives in self-talk—the voice in your head that comments on everything you do. If that voice is always negative, you might accept it as truth. But you can learn to change it:

1. **Notice the Negativity**
   Pay attention when you find yourself saying, "I am not good enough," or "I will fail."
2. **Challenge It**
   Ask, "Is this really true? Do I have proof?" Often, you may see that your self-talk is exaggerated or based on old fears.

3. **Replace with Balanced Statements**
   Instead of "I am worthless," try, "I have strengths and weaknesses, just like everyone." You do not have to force yourself to say, "I am amazing." Aim for a middle ground that feels realistic yet more positive.

Over time, this practice can soften shame's grip.

12.7 Seeking Forgiveness from Others—and Yourself

Guilt often arises from something you did that hurt someone else. If that is the case, apologizing sincerely can be part of the healing. A proper apology has these elements:

- **Acknowledgment**: Clearly state what you did wrong.
- **Regret**: Express that you feel bad about it.
- **Responsibility**: Do not blame others or make excuses.
- **Plan for Change**: Explain how you will avoid repeating the mistake.

However, even if the other person accepts your apology, you might still feel guilt. That is when you need to forgive yourself. Remember that everyone makes errors. Dwelling on them does not undo them; learning from them is what matters.

12.8 Shame vs. Motivation

Some men believe shame or guilt can push them to improve. While mild guilt might motivate you to correct course, deep shame tends to sap your energy rather than fuel it. If you believe you are fundamentally flawed, you might think, "What is the point of trying?" On the other hand, if you see your actions as fixable, you can channel your guilt into positive changes.

- **Ask Yourself**: "Is this feeling pushing me to do better, or making me feel helpless?"
- **Focus on Action**: "What specific step can I take to address this issue?"
- **Seek Support**: If you are trapped in a shame spiral, talk to a friend or counselor for an outside perspective.

12.9 Dealing with Cultural or Family Pressures

In some families or cultures, men are expected to never show vulnerability. They might be told to "man up" or "stop whining" if they express sadness or regret. This can create shame around normal human emotions.

- **Question the Message**: Does being a man truly mean never admitting mistakes or pain? Many would argue that true strength includes honesty about faults.
- **Find Safe Spaces**: Seek out people or groups who support open emotional expression. This could be friends, a mentor, or a men's group that encourages growth.
- **Set Boundaries**: If relatives constantly shame you for not meeting outdated standards, limit how much you let their words shape your self-image. You can still respect them but follow your own healthier path.

12.10 Methods for Coping with Overwhelming Shame or Guilt

1. **Writing It Out**
   Journaling can help you identify patterns. Write down the situation, how you felt, and any thoughts that came up. Sometimes seeing your words on paper makes them clearer.
2. **Talking to a Professional**
   Therapists are trained to help people untangle deep guilt or shame. A counselor can guide you through past experiences and help you develop healthier coping tools.
3. **Mindfulness Techniques**
   Practices like gentle breathing or focusing on the present moment can reduce the storm of negative thoughts. Over time, you learn to observe your feelings without being overwhelmed.
4. **Support Groups**
   Hearing other men share similar struggles can normalize your experience. You may realize you are not alone or "defective" for feeling this way.

12.11 Setting Realistic Standards

Sometimes shame grows because your standards are so high that any slip feels disastrous. For instance, if you believe you must always be the perfect husband, father, or employee, the moment you fail at one small task, shame kicks in. Adjusting expectations can help:

- **Remember Human Limits**: No one can be perfect. Mistakes are part of the learning process.
- **Break Down Goals**: Instead of "I must be a top performer every single day," aim for steady improvement. Celebrate small steps.
- **Allow Breaks**: Overwork can heighten mistakes and guilt. Plan for rest so you can recharge.

12.12 When Shame is Tied to Trauma

Some men carry shame from traumatic events—such as abuse, violence, or serious neglect. Trauma can make a person feel "damaged" or "at fault," even if they were the victim. Coping with trauma-related shame often requires specialized help. A counselor skilled in trauma can introduce methods to break the cycle of self-blame. These might include certain therapies that help reframe how you see your past and process lingering emotional pain.

12.13 Rebuilding Self-Worth

Overcoming shame is partly about rebuilding trust in yourself. This process can involve:

- **Noticing Strengths**: Reflect on what you do well or how you have helped others. Your shame might hide these positives from your view.
- **Accepting Compliments**: If you typically dismiss praise, practice simply saying, "Thank you." Over time, you may internalize the positive feedback.
- **Engaging in Acts of Kindness**: Helping others can boost a sense of worth. Even small acts—like volunteering or assisting a neighbor—remind you that you have value.

- **Working Toward Goals**: Pick a realistic personal goal. Each step toward it demonstrates you are capable, helping to counter "I can't do anything right" thoughts.

12.14 Supporting a Friend Who Feels Shame or Guilt

If a friend confides that they feel deep shame or guilt, you can offer supportive words:

1. **Listen Without Judgment**
   Let them speak. Avoid interrupting with quick fixes.
2. **Acknowledge Their Emotions**
   Say, "That sounds tough," or "I understand you feel really bad about this."
3. **Encourage Them to Seek Help**
   Suggest talking to a counselor or support group if the feelings are severe.
4. **Remind Them of Their Good Qualities**
   They might be stuck in negative self-view. Gently point out strengths or times they succeeded.

12.15 The Relationship between Shame, Guilt, and Anger

Sometimes shame or guilt appears as anger. A man who feels worthless might lash out to mask those underlying feelings. Recognizing this link can help de-escalate conflicts (as discussed in Chapter 11). If you notice yourself or another person becoming disproportionately angry, consider whether shame or guilt might be fueling the fire. Addressing the root cause can stop the anger from spiraling.

12.16 Forgiving Yourself After Conflict

Earlier chapters discussed how conflicts can happen at work or home. When we handle them poorly—saying cruel words or making a big scene—we might regret our actions later. The result can be guilt or shame. The steps to move forward include:

- **Owning Up**: Apologize to those affected. Show genuine remorse.
- **Reflect on the Cause**: Were you stressed, frustrated, or feeling threatened? Recognize the trigger so you can manage it better next time.
- **Plan for Future**: Outline how you will respond if you feel anger rising again. Maybe you take a short walk, breathe deeply, or pause to gather thoughts before speaking.
- **Let Go**: Once you have done what you can to fix the harm, continuing to beat yourself up does not help. Resolve to do better and focus on the present.

12.17 Healthy Boundaries against External Shame

Sometimes shame comes from people who try to put you down or control you. If you have someone in your life who constantly criticizes or humiliates you:

- **Speak Up**: Politely but firmly say their comments are not acceptable.
- **Limit Contact**: If they keep doing it, reduce how often you interact or how much personal info you share with them.
- **Seek Support**: Friends or counselors can help you process the negative impact of toxic people.
- **Remember Your Value**: One person's harsh view is not an absolute truth. Surround yourself with those who treat you well.

12.18 Turning Shame and Guilt into Positive Growth

Sometimes, these emotions hold lessons. If you feel guilty about not spending time with your kids, this might push you to plan more family activities. If you feel shame about your job performance, you might decide to acquire new skills. The key is to address the root issue rather than drowning in self-blame.

- **Identify the Lesson**: Ask yourself what this guilt or shame can teach you.
- **Take Action**: Put that lesson into a specific plan—like scheduling dedicated family time or enrolling in a course to improve work skills.
- **Track Progress**: Check if these changes ease your feelings of guilt or shame. If they do, you know you are on the right track.

12.19 Patience and Persistence

Overcoming deep shame or guilt does not happen in one day. It is often a gradual process with setbacks along the way. Some days, you might feel confident and free, while other days, old negative thoughts creep back.

- **Accept the Ups and Downs**: Change usually follows a bumpy path. Do not be discouraged if you slip into old thinking now and then.
- **Use Relapses as Learning**: If you find yourself stuck in shame again, note what triggered it. You might discover new tools to handle that trigger next time.
- **Celebrate Small Wins**: When you handle a situation differently than before—maybe apologizing quickly or standing up for yourself—recognize that progress.

12.20 Conclusion of Chapter 12

Shame and guilt can have a powerful hold on men, shaping how they see themselves and how they act in relationships or conflicts. But these feelings do not need to define you forever. By understanding where they come from, distinguishing between healthy and unhealthy guilt, and adopting strategies to challenge negative self-talk, you can break free from their grip.

This journey might involve self-reflection, apologies, therapy, or simply practicing kindness toward yourself. In the end, the goal is to see mistakes as events to learn from, not as proof of being worthless. Releasing shame and guilt helps you approach life with a clearer mind, better relationships, and a stronger sense of self.

In the next chapters (13 and 14), we will move on to building on these emotional understandings by looking at how to achieve personal goals (Chapter 13) and how reflection can spark growth (Chapter 14). By continually adding new insights, we can create a framework for personal development that addresses both your inner feelings and outward actions.

CHAPTER 13

Achieving Personal Goals

Introduction
Personal goals are targets or objectives you set for yourself to improve your life. They may involve health, career, finances, creativity, or relationships. Men often carry many hopes, but not all succeed in turning these dreams into reality. Sometimes, the problem is not a lack of ability but rather a lack of clear planning or consistent follow-through. This chapter provides practical advice for defining, organizing, and reaching personal goals in a balanced way.

We will look at how to select goals that match your desires, arrange them into workable steps, keep track of progress, and stay motivated through tough periods. By using these ideas, you can avoid confusion and frustration and instead stay on a path that leads to real results. Whether you want to pick up a new skill, make a career change, or improve a part of your daily life, the tools in this chapter can help you move forward in an organized manner.

13.1 Why Goals Matter

Some people go through life reacting to events rather than guiding them. While flexibility can be beneficial, having no goals can result in feeling lost. Goals help you set your sights on something meaningful, giving you a reason to push on even when faced with obstacles. They act as a sort of compass, pointing you toward improvements and achievements that matter to you.

- **Sense of Purpose**: A clear personal goal can give you something to look forward to each day. Instead of drifting, you have direction.
- **Structure**: Well-defined goals let you create a schedule or plan. This structure helps you manage time and resources effectively.
- **Motivation**: When you know what you are aiming for, it can be easier to keep going, especially if progress is visible.
- **Personal Growth**: Achieving a goal usually requires new knowledge or better habits, which contribute to your overall development.

Having a goal does not mean ignoring fun or relaxation. Instead, it means striking a balance between living in the moment and working consistently toward something you value.

13.2 Choosing the Right Goals

Picking the wrong goals—or goals based on someone else's wishes—can cause low motivation. Men sometimes adopt targets they do not truly care about, simply because they think they "should." For example, a man may believe he must climb the corporate ladder because his peers do, when he might actually prefer a different career path.

1. **Look at Your Values**: Think about what really matters to you. Is it freedom, helping others, security for your family, or creative expression? Align your goals with these core values.
2. **Reflect on Your Strengths**: Goals can stretch you, but it is also wise to consider areas where you have some ability or interest. If you hate numbers, making a goal to become an accountant might be an uphill battle.
3. **Ask "Why?"**: Before committing, ask why you want this. If the reason feels forced—like pleasing family or society—pause and see if you can adjust the goal to fit your genuine interests.

By choosing goals that genuinely speak to you, you increase the chance of steady motivation and success.

13.3 Making Goals Specific and Measurable

Vague targets, like "I want to get healthier," can be hard to track. Instead, shape your goals in a way that clarifies what success looks like. A popular format often recommended is "S.M.A.R.T.": Specific, Measurable, Attainable, Relevant, and Time-bound. While you do not have to follow this strictly, it highlights the importance of detail.

- **Specific**: Clearly state what you want. For instance, "I will lose 10 pounds" or "I will learn to play 3 songs on the guitar."

- **Measurable**: Identify a way to gauge progress, such as pounds lost, songs learned, or a test score improved.
- **Attainable**: Ensure the goal is within reach. Aiming to lose 10 pounds in 2 weeks may be too extreme, while aiming for that over a few months is more realistic.
- **Relevant**: Connect it to your life or values. If you do not really value a certain fitness goal, you might not keep pushing.
- **Time-bound**: Set a deadline or time frame—"by the end of the year" or "within 3 months."

This clarity helps you break down goals into chunks you can track.

13.4 Breaking Down Large Goals into Steps

Big objectives can feel intimidating. If you look at the entire mountain at once, it is easy to feel overwhelmed. Breaking a large goal into smaller tasks can reduce this stress and help you see steady progress.

- **Brainstorm All Tasks**: Write every little thing you can think of that might be needed. For example, if your goal is to start a side business, list tasks like "research market," "design a logo," "build a website," "decide pricing," "register the business," and so on.
- **Organize into Phases**: Group related tasks. Perhaps Phase 1 is research, Phase 2 is branding, Phase 3 is launching, etc.
- **Set Mini-Deadlines**: Assign approximate completion times for each smaller task. This prevents procrastination and gives you milestones to celebrate.

Seeing a big goal as a series of steps makes it less scary. It also makes it clearer when you are on schedule or falling behind.

13.5 Time Management for Goal Pursuit

You can have the best goals, but if you do not arrange your schedule to work on them, progress will be slow. Men often juggle work duties, family responsibilities, and personal errands. Making time for personal goals requires conscious effort:

1. **Calendar Blocks**: Reserve specific periods in your calendar for goal tasks. Treat these blocks like important appointments.
2. **Set Priorities**: If you cannot tackle everything in a day, choose your top tasks first. Doing the most important or most urgent tasks early gives you a better chance of completion.
3. **Delegate or Drop**: Look at your to-do list. Are there tasks you can assign to someone else, or stop doing entirely? Sometimes, stepping back from non-essential duties frees up space for more meaningful goals.
4. **Reduce Distractions**: Social media, random web browsing, and unnecessary phone checks can eat up a surprising amount of time. Identify your common distractions and decide how you will reduce them.

Time management is about quality, not just quantity. Two hours of focused work on your goal each day can be more productive than five hours of scattered, distracted effort.

13.6 Staying Motivated When Progress Is Slow

Some goals—like learning a new language or saving enough money for a large purchase—can take months or even years. You may feel enthusiastic at first, but as the days go by, motivation might drop. Here are some tips:

- **Remember Your "Why"**: Write down or recall the reason behind your goal. Visualize the result you want to achieve. This mental reminder can boost your willpower.
- **Track Success**: Keep a journal, chart, or digital tracker to log each small accomplishment. Seeing evidence of growth, even if small, can keep you pushing forward.
- **Reward Yourself**: After hitting a milestone, treat yourself in a healthy way. This might be taking a relaxing day off, getting a new book, or enjoying a favorite meal.
- **Seek Support**: Share your goals with a friend or join a group that has similar objectives. Encouragement from others can lift your spirits when you feel stuck.

No one stays motivated 100% of the time. The key is developing habits that keep you going even on days when your energy is low.

13.7 Coping with Obstacles and Setbacks

Rarely do goals unfold without a hitch. You might encounter a financial hurdle, a health problem, or a sudden shift in your schedule. Rather than viewing these as failures, treat them as challenges to work around.

1. **Stay Flexible**: If your original plan does not fit the new circumstances, adjust it. Changing a goal's timeline or approach can be better than quitting entirely.
2. **Problem-Solve**: Ask, "What options do I have now?" or "Who can help me figure this out?" Often, brainstorming solutions with others can reveal paths you had not considered.
3. **Focus on What You Can Control**: You cannot control every external factor. But you can manage your reactions, your attitude, and how much effort you put in.
4. **Stay Hopeful**: Remind yourself that a setback does not erase all progress. Many successful men have faced failures or detours before reaching their aims.

Obstacles can sometimes sharpen your skills. They force you to adapt, learn, and come out stronger, as long as you do not let them stop you permanently.

13.8 The Role of Accountability

Telling someone about your goal can make it feel more real. Accountability can come from friends, relatives, mentors, or even a professional coach. The idea is that you periodically report progress, making it less tempting to let tasks slide.

- **Accountability Partner**: This can be a friend who also has goals. You meet or message each other weekly to discuss wins, struggles, and next steps.
- **Group Settings**: Classes or clubs focused on certain skills (like coding or fitness) provide natural accountability. Everyone is on the same path, cheering each other on.
- **Online Platforms**: There are apps where you set tasks and check them off in a shared space, letting others see your progress.
- **Mentors or Coaches**: A mentor can offer insights and keep you on track with reminders and advice.

Finding at least one person or group to keep you accountable can significantly boost your consistency.

13.9 Balancing Multiple Goals

It is common to have more than one goal at the same time. Perhaps you want to improve your physical health, learn a new skill, and increase your savings. While being ambitious is good, juggling too many goals can lead to burnout or divided focus.

- **Rank Your Goals**: Determine which one is most urgent or valuable. This top goal should get the majority of your time.
- **Set Time Blocks**: Maybe you spend mornings on your main goal and weekends on a secondary goal.
- **Be Realistic**: If you only have an hour a day of free time, consider whether you can truly tackle three or four major goals at once. It might be more effective to concentrate on one or two until you gain momentum, then add others.

A gradual approach keeps you from getting overwhelmed and dropping everything.

13.10 Overcoming Fear of Failure

For many men, fear of not succeeding can hold them back from even starting. This fear can arise from past failures, high expectations, or worry about what others might think. Here is how to challenge that fear:

1. **Focus on the Process**: Instead of obsessing over the end result, pay attention to daily or weekly tasks. This shifts your mind from outcome anxiety to manageable actions.
2. **Embrace Mistakes as Learning**: Each slip-up or shortfall can teach you something, whether it is how to plan better or which approaches do not work.
3. **Visualize Success**: Spend a few moments imagining how you will feel when you achieve your target. Let that positive emotion balance out the fear.

4. **Speak Kindly to Yourself**: Harsh inner criticism can freeze you. Remind yourself that everyone experiences setbacks and that trying is itself a big step.

Failure is part of growth. It is not a permanent condition but rather feedback on what to change or improve.

13.11 Celebrating Small Milestones—Without Overusing Time or Money

While you must avoid certain words, we can note the importance of acknowledging small achievements on the way to a bigger goal. This does not mean throwing a big party or spending lots of money each time. Instead, pick modest ways to mark your progress:

- **Share the Update**: Tell a close friend or family member that you hit a milestone. Hearing their supportive feedback can lift your mood.
- **Enjoy Simple Pleasures**: Maybe you decide to watch a favorite movie, go for a quiet walk, or treat yourself to a favorite snack—while keeping it reasonable.
- **Reflect on the Effort**: Spend a few minutes thinking about how you overcame challenges. This reflection can reinforce your confidence that you can handle bigger steps next.

A balanced approach helps you avoid feeling deprived while keeping you responsible.

13.12 Finding Inspiration from Others

Reading about or talking to men who have reached similar targets can fuel your own drive. You can learn from their strategies, mistakes, and breakthroughs. This does not mean you must copy them exactly, but you can adapt tips to your own situation.

- **Biographies and Interviews**: Many successful people share how they overcame hurdles and stayed persistent.

- **Online Forums or Groups**: Find a community where people with similar interests share tips or successes.
- **Local Groups and Workshops**: Face-to-face events can create real connections and provide ongoing encouragement.

Seeing real-life examples reminds you that progress is possible, even if the process takes time and requires persistence.

13.13 Handling Self-Doubt

It is natural to occasionally wonder if you can achieve what you set out to do. Self-doubt can creep in, especially if you are trying something new or have had setbacks in the past. Here are some methods to manage those thoughts:

1. **Collect Evidence of Past Success**: Recall other times you overcame hurdles. Write them down. This proof of prior victories can lessen new doubts.
2. **Break Down the Task**: The more you see small steps, the less intimidating the overall goal seems.
3. **Use Positive Role Models**: Remind yourself of people who started from a similar point and succeeded. If they could do it, it is at least possible for you.
4. **Seek Encouragement**: Talk to a trusted friend who can remind you of your strengths. Sometimes an outside voice helps counter your own negative chatter.

Doubts may never vanish fully, but you can learn to keep moving forward despite them.

13.14 Dealing with Criticism from Others

Not everyone will applaud your ambitions. Sometimes, friends or family might express doubts about your goals. They might say, "You are wasting your time" or "That is unrealistic." While feedback can be helpful, it can also discourage you if it is negative or not based on facts.

- **Consider the Source**: Does this person have expertise in the area, or are they just being negative?
- **Filter Helpful Advice**: Even critical comments may contain useful points. If there is something constructive you can use, apply it.
- **Avoid Argument**: Getting into heated debates about your goals can sap your energy. Politely state you value their concern but maintain your decision if you still believe in it.
- **Find Support Elsewhere**: If certain people are constantly negative, balance that by talking to those who encourage you in productive ways.

Remember that your goals are yours. You can listen to others, but ultimately, you decide your path.

13.15 Monitoring and Reviewing Progress

Setting a plan is just one part of the process. Regularly checking how you are doing is equally important. You might discover you are ahead of schedule in one area but lagging in another.

- **Weekly or Monthly Check-Ins**: Block off time to review what you did in the past period. Note where you succeeded and where you fell short.
- **Adjust if Needed**: If you find you underestimated how long tasks take, modify your timeline. If you realized you are not as interested in one aspect of your goal, see if you can replace or revise it.
- **Stay Honest**: Hiding from the truth because you do not like the numbers or results will not help you make changes. Face the facts, then plan your next move.

Regular review times keep you focused and help you correct course early, rather than discovering big issues right before your deadline.

13.16 The Connection Between Physical Health and Personal Goals

Men often overlook how important physical health is for success in other areas. Lack of energy or stress can slow you down. If you are constantly tired or unwell, working toward your goal becomes more difficult.

- **Exercise and Movement**: Regular activity improves your mood, energy, and mental clarity. This helps you stay consistent in your tasks.
- **Good Nutrition**: A balanced diet can prevent slumps in energy. Avoid relying on sugar or junk food for quick boosts, as the crash afterward can reduce productivity.
- **Adequate Rest**: Sleep is not a luxury; it is vital. A rested brain is more creative and better at problem-solving.

Taking care of your body forms a strong base for tackling personal goals.

13.17 Recognizing Burnout and Taking Breaks

Men sometimes believe they must power through without any pause. While dedication is commendable, not allowing breaks can lead to burnout—a state of exhaustion where motivation crashes and small tasks feel too big.

- **Know the Signs**: If you feel constantly drained, irritable, or uninterested in tasks you used to enjoy, you might be burned out.
- **Schedule Downtime**: Brief daily breaks or restful weekend activities can recharge your mind.
- **Balance**: Sometimes stepping away from your goal briefly can renew enthusiasm. Then you return with fresh eyes and new ideas.

A short break does not mean you are abandoning your goal. It is an investment in your long-term capacity to keep going.

13.18 Changing Goals When Priorities Shift

Your life situation may change due to a new job, family growth, or evolving interests. In such cases, you may feel conflicted about old goals that no longer fit. It is okay to alter or replace them.

- **Reflect on the New Reality**: Ask if the goal still aligns with your values and day-to-day life.
- **Adjust the Scope**: Maybe you reduce the scale of the goal or change the timeline.

- **Let Go if Needed**: If a goal no longer serves you, freeing yourself from it can create space for a better choice.

Being adaptable does not mean you quit easily; it means you respect your changing life path and find goals that still resonate.

13.19 The Importance of Self-Confidence

Without a baseline of self-belief, you might give up the first time you face a roadblock. Self-confidence is built by small achievements, kind self-talk, and proof that you can overcome challenges. Each time you successfully complete a step, you add a brick to your foundation of confidence.

- **Celebrate Progress**: Pause and acknowledge each milestone. Let that success feed into your sense of capability.
- **Stay Humble**: Confidence does not mean arrogance. It means trusting your ability to learn and adapt, not that you know everything already.
- **Push Your Limits Gently**: Sometimes, do things that are a bit beyond your comfort zone. Overcoming these mini-challenges shows you can tackle bigger ones later.

13.20 Conclusion of Chapter 13

Achieving personal goals is not magic—it involves clear definition, steady planning, and ongoing effort. By selecting goals that match your values, shaping them into specific tasks, and managing your time effectively, you can see real changes in your life. Along the way, obstacles will test your resolve, but with the right tools—like breaking down tasks, seeking accountability, and staying flexible—you can push through roadblocks.

Motivation may fluctuate, and you might need to adapt or even swap goals as your life evolves. This is normal. The main idea is to keep your intentions lined up with who you are and what you truly care about. In the next chapter, we will explore the power of reflection for growth. Reflection helps you learn from both successes and failures, making future goal-setting and self-improvement even more efficient. With clear aims, consistent action, and a spirit of learning, you can set yourself on a path of continuous progress.

CHAPTER 14

Growth Through Reflection

Introduction

Reflection is the act of looking inward to understand your thoughts, experiences, and behaviors. Many men focus on action and external achievements, but taking time to process what has happened—both good and bad—offers invaluable insights. By reflecting, you spot patterns, uncover lessons from mistakes, and reinforce positive behaviors. This chapter dives into practical methods for reflection, showing how it can boost personal growth and well-being.

We will look at why reflection is often overlooked, how to practice it, and ways to use it to sharpen your skills and emotional stability. Reflection is not about dwelling on regrets or daydreaming aimlessly. Instead, it is about honest evaluation of your day-to-day life so you can adjust as needed. Whether you are reviewing a work project, a family interaction, or a health habit, systematic reflection helps you see where you can improve or what you should keep doing.

14.1 Why Reflection Matters

By thinking carefully about your actions and emotions, you build self-awareness. This helps you make better decisions in the future. Instead of repeating errors, you can catch them early or replace them with more productive behavior. Reflection also deepens your understanding of yourself—your strengths, triggers, and preferences.

- **Identify Patterns**: You may realize you always get upset in certain conditions, or that you are at your most creative in the mornings.
- **Reinforce Good Habits**: Noting which habits led to successes can encourage you to keep them.
- **Handle Emotions**: Reflection can uncover hidden feelings, letting you address them before they cause bigger issues.
- **Boost Confidence**: When you see that you have learned from past mistakes, you trust your ability to handle what comes next.

While some men see reflection as "sitting around thinking," it is actually a powerful tool for guiding personal growth.

14.2 Barriers to Reflection

Despite its benefits, many men do not reflect regularly. Common reasons include:

1. **Lack of Time**: Schedules packed with work and errands leave little room for quiet thought.
2. **Fear of Painful Insights**: Reflecting might reveal guilt, shame, or the need to admit past errors.
3. **Focus on Action**: Some men equate doing with progress, ignoring the value of planning or reviewing.
4. **Discomfort with Emotions**: Reflection often involves confronting feelings, which can feel awkward if you are not used to it.

Recognizing these barriers helps you address them. You can choose a shorter reflection method or build a small daily or weekly practice that fits your routine.

14.3 Creating a Reflection Routine

A routine makes reflection part of your life rather than a random occurrence. Even 10 or 15 minutes can make a difference if you use that time effectively. Here are some ideas:

- **End-of-Day Reflection**: Spend a few minutes before bed noting key events or thoughts. Ask, "What went well today? What was challenging?"
- **Weekly Review**: Once a week, go deeper. Write down highlights, obstacles, and lessons. Look ahead to next week and set intentions.
- **Quiet Mornings**: Some men wake up earlier than necessary to have a silent moment for reading, thinking, or journaling. This can set a calm tone for the day.

The best routine is the one you can actually maintain. Start small, and if it fits well, extend it.

14.4 Journaling as a Reflection Tool

Keeping a journal is a popular way to process your experiences. Writing your thoughts forces you to slow down and clarify them, which can reveal new insights. It also leaves a record you can revisit later.

1. **Simple Approach**: Dedicate a page to daily reflections—what happened, how you felt, what you learned. This can be done in 5 to 10 minutes.
2. **Detailed Approach**: If you have time, write about specific problems, emotional shifts, or future ideas. Ask yourself why events happened the way they did and how you can react differently next time.
3. **Prompt-Based**: Use questions or prompts like "What did I do today that I am proud of?" or "Where could I improve tomorrow?"
4. **Review**: Every few weeks or months, read old entries. You might see patterns or progress you never noticed before.

A journal does not have to be fancy. A simple notebook or a digital file works fine. The key is consistency and honesty.

14.5 Reflecting on Goals and Progress

In the previous chapter, we looked at setting and reaching personal goals. Reflection ties closely to that process because it allows you to check whether your methods are effective and if the goal still aligns with your values.

- **Ask "What Worked?"**: When you hit a milestone or succeed at a step, note which habits or approaches helped.
- **Ask "What Did Not Work?"**: If you missed a deadline, figure out the root cause. Was it poor planning, lack of motivation, or an unexpected event?
- **Adjust Accordingly**: Use these insights to refine your plan. If you discovered you are too tired after work for a certain task, move it to a morning slot.
- **Celebrate Progress**: Recognizing that you have completed certain steps can keep your motivation strong.

Reflection keeps you from blindly pushing forward without learning from the day-to-day challenges that arise when chasing a goal.

14.6 Learning from Failure

Mistakes and missteps are often seen as negatives, but through reflection, they can become stepping stones to better behavior. Failing at something—whether it is a test, a business venture, or a personal challenge—can be an opportunity if you do not let shame or despair take over.

1. **Detach from Emotion**: Let the initial wave of disappointment pass. Then calmly analyze what went wrong.
2. **Own Your Part**: There might be external factors, but also acknowledge where your choices or preparation fell short.
3. **Extract Lessons**: Ask, "What could I do differently next time?" or "What skills or resources did I lack?"
4. **Try Again**: Implement these lessons in a future attempt. If the same approach keeps failing, reflection can guide you toward new approaches.

Failure is natural, but repeating the same mistakes without learning wastes an opportunity to grow.

14.7 Reflecting on Relationships

Whether family, friends, or romantic partners, relationships shape a big part of a man's life. Reflection can help you see how you interact, communicate, and handle conflict with loved ones.

- **Communication Check**: Think about recent talks. Did you really listen? Did you express your thoughts clearly? Were there moments you wish you had handled differently?
- **Conflict Handling**: Recall disagreements. Did you keep your cool, or did anger take control? Reflect on what triggered you and how you might prevent or reduce that next time.
- **Time Spent Together**: Reflect on how much quality time you share with important people. If you realize you have been neglecting them, plan ways to reconnect.
- **Boundaries and Needs**: Notice if you feel drained or taken advantage of. Reflection can reveal where you need to set more balanced boundaries.

This type of reflection can strengthen your connections and prevent small tensions from growing into major issues.

14.8 Mindful Practices

Mindfulness is the practice of being fully present in the moment. This can include focusing on your breathing, the sensations in your body, or the details of your surroundings. Such practices often naturally lead to reflection because they slow down racing thoughts.

1. **Short Mindful Sessions**: Sit quietly for a few minutes, pay attention to inhaling and exhaling, and notice when your mind drifts. Gently bring it back.
2. **Mindful Activities**: Wash dishes, go for a walk, or eat a meal with full awareness of smells, textures, and tastes.
3. **Combine with Reflection**: After a mindful session, ask yourself how you feel, what thoughts came up, and what changes you can make in your actions or outlook.

By getting in touch with the present, you can more easily see what is working or not in your life.

14.9 Using Technology to Aid Reflection

Modern devices can distract us, but they can also support reflection if used wisely:

- **Apps for Journaling**: Some apps allow you to make daily entries, add mood tracking, or set reminders to write.
- **Meditation Apps**: Guided sessions can help you quiet your mind and notice your thoughts.
- **Habit-Tracking Tools**: By marking completed tasks or healthy habits, you can look back and see patterns.
- **Online Communities**: Group forums for personal growth can offer prompts or questions to reflect on each day or week.

However, be cautious not to let technology become a substitute for genuine introspection. The key is using it as a helper, not a crutch.

14.10 Reflection at Work

Work is where many men spend a large part of their day. Reflecting on tasks, projects, and workplace interactions can improve performance and reduce stress.

- **End-of-Workday Review**: Write down or think about what you accomplished, what got in your way, and how you felt. This helps you plan for tomorrow.
- **Project Post-Mortems**: After completing a major project, gather the team (or do a solo review if you work alone) to discuss what went well and what did not. Document lessons learned.
- **Feedback Integration**: If you receive feedback from a boss or colleague, reflect on it honestly. Even if you disagree, try to see if there is a kernel of truth you can use.

Continual reflection at work helps you identify patterns in productivity, collaboration, and job satisfaction.

14.11 Reflecting on Emotional Well-Being

Men sometimes push aside emotions, but this can lead to hidden stress or mounting tension. Reflection can bring these feelings into the open, where they can be managed more constructively.

- **Identify Stress Points**: Did something make you feel anxious or angry? Reflect on why it bothered you. Was it the content of someone's words, the tone, or a personal trigger?
- **Check Moods Regularly**: Some men keep a simple "mood diary," rating how they feel each day. Over time, patterns emerge—maybe stress spikes on Mondays or after certain events.
- **Plan Coping Strategies**: If you see a recurring source of stress, plan ways to handle it better (e.g., short breaks, talking to a friend, or adjusting your environment).
- **Accept Both Positive and Negative Feelings**: Reflection is not just for problems. Notice moments of happiness or pride, too, so you can repeat the behaviors that led there.

Understanding emotions keeps them from silently controlling your actions.

14.12 Group or Partner Reflection

Reflecting does not have to be a solo activity. Sometimes talking with a trusted friend or group can deepen insights. By sharing your perspectives and listening to theirs, you may see angles you missed.

- **Support Circles**: Some men form small groups where members meet regularly to discuss life goals, challenges, and lessons learned.
- **Mentoring Arrangements**: A mentor can ask guiding questions that prompt you to reflect more carefully.
- **Family Reflection**: Even brief family meetings to talk about what went well during the week and where improvements are needed can bond everyone together.

The main caution is to choose people who can maintain confidentiality and offer balanced feedback, rather than being overly critical or dismissive.

14.13 Reflecting on Personal Development Over Time

Men grow and change as years pass. Reflecting on long-term progress can give you a sense of achievement or highlight areas that need renewed effort.

- **Past vs. Present**: Compare your skills, habits, or mindset from 5 years ago to today. Are you more patient, more confident, or more prepared to handle challenges?
- **Life Milestones**: Look at key events—graduation, starting a job, becoming a parent—and how each event shifted your priorities or beliefs.
- **Future Plans**: After seeing how far you have come, you can guess where you might want to be in another 5 or 10 years. This can lead to new goals or affirm your current path.

Long-term reflection connects your past with your future, providing a sense of continuity and purpose.

14.14 Avoiding Overthinking

Though reflection is useful, it can turn into overthinking if you dwell on the same problem without taking action. Overthinking can spiral into anxiety, self-doubt, or procrastination. To prevent that:

- **Set Time Limits**: If you find yourself ruminating, give yourself a set period—maybe 10 or 15 minutes—to think it through, then move on or do a small action that addresses the concern.
- **Take Small Steps**: If you cannot decide on a big move, pick a minor test or experiment. Doing something helps break the loop of constant pondering.
- **Shift Focus**: Engage in a quick activity—like cleaning up your workspace or taking a short walk—to reset your mental state.

Reflection should lead to better self-understanding and improvement, not freezing in uncertainty.

14.15 Reflection Aids Decision-Making

When men face major choices—such as switching careers, moving to a new city, or starting a family—reflection can clarify the pros and cons. By writing out or thinking through the potential outcomes, you reduce the chance of impulsive decisions driven by short-term feelings.

- **List of Pros and Cons**: Classic but effective. See your options in front of you.
- **Visualize Outcomes**: Imagine how daily life might look if you pick one option over the other.
- **Consult Trusted People**: Their perspectives can feed into your reflection, offering angles you had not considered.
- **Trust Your Values**: If an option clashes with your fundamental beliefs, that is a sign it might not be right for you.

This approach builds confidence that you picked the best path possible with the information you had, even if challenges arise later.

14.16 Spiritual or Philosophical Reflection

For some men, reflection includes spiritual or philosophical aspects. This might involve prayer, meditation, or simply pondering big questions about purpose and meaning. These practices can add a deeper layer to personal growth, providing a sense of connection beyond daily tasks.

- **Read Inspiring Texts**: Whether they are religious scriptures or secular philosophies, reading such works can prompt meaningful questions about your life.
- **Quiet Retreats**: Some choose to go on weekend retreats or take time off in a peaceful environment, away from routine distractions.
- **Write Down Insights**: If a specific insight or piece of wisdom moves you, note it in a separate section of your journal. Revisit these notes when you need a guiding principle.

This optional layer of reflection can bring calm and direction, even if you are not part of a formal religious or spiritual group.

14.17 Reflection on Self-Care and Balance

Reflection can also highlight areas where you are neglecting your own needs. Men sometimes push themselves too hard or ignore signs of stress, only to burn out later.

- **Energy Levels**: Reflect on how you feel each morning and evening. Notice if you are constantly exhausted.
- **Mental Breaks**: Are you giving yourself short pauses during the day or using every spare moment for more tasks?
- **Relaxing Activities**: Do you have at least one hobby or pursuit that helps you unwind? If not, reflection can remind you to include something enjoyable in your schedule.
- **Physical Warning Signs**: Headaches, muscle tension, and trouble sleeping can all signal stress that needs addressing.

Monitoring self-care keeps you from pushing past healthy limits.

14.18 Self-Evaluation vs. Self-Criticism

When reflecting, it is easy to slip into harsh self-judgment if you are not meeting certain standards. While honest evaluation is good, beating yourself up leads to shame and discouragement (as discussed in Chapter 12).

- **Focus on Facts**: "I missed the deadline" is a fact. "I am completely worthless" is an exaggeration.
- **Practice Self-Compassion**: Treat yourself with the same kindness you would offer a friend in the same situation.
- **Look Forward**: After noting what went wrong, shift to "How can I correct or avoid this next time?"
- **Remember Successes**: Balance out any negative points with reminders of times you did well.

This balanced view allows you to grow without tearing yourself down.

14.19 Putting Reflection into Action

Reflection is not meant to stay in your mind or on paper. The real impact comes when you apply insights in daily life.

1. **List Action Items**: For each insight—like recognizing you get distracted by social media—write a practical step, such as setting app limits.
2. **Set Timelines**: If you reflect on a skill you want to improve, schedule a practice session or online course.
3. **Check Results**: After trying an action, reflect again to see if it helped. This loops reflection back into continual improvement.
4. **Share with Accountability Partner**: Telling someone about your plan can help you stick to it.

By converting reflection into doable steps, you ensure that your introspection leads to meaningful progress.

14.20 Conclusion of Chapter 14

Reflection is a quiet force for growth. It allows you to learn from daily experiences, manage emotions more skillfully, and fine-tune your path. While men are sometimes expected to keep emotions tucked away or to stay constantly busy, setting aside time to think about your life can bring clarity and direction. By journaling, mindful observation, or group discussions, you deepen self-awareness and discover patterns that shape better decisions.

This chapter showed that reflection can help you in various areas—your personal goals, your work, and your relationships—leading to a more purposeful life. You do not need a lot of fancy methods. Simple, consistent moments of introspection can have a profound effect. As we continue to Chapters 15 and 16, we will look at specific ways to find motivation and handle stress, both of which connect strongly with the practice of reflection. By keeping a reflective mindset, you ensure that every step you take is informed by past lessons, paving the way for steady personal development.

CHAPTER 15

Practical Ways to Find Motivation

Introduction
Motivation is often described as the drive that moves you to act. It influences whether you start a project, persist through obstacles, or give up at the first sign of trouble. Men sometimes face unique motivational barriers, including fear of failure, external pressures, or simply feeling stuck in a routine. This chapter will present practical tools for finding the internal energy that pushes you forward. Rather than offering grand theories, we will focus on clear methods that you can use daily or weekly. From the importance of setting inspiring goals to creating a personal encouragement system, these methods can help keep your motivation strong in both your personal and professional life.

Having a consistent sense of drive can lead to better achievements, but more importantly, it can support a sense of well-being. Feeling motivated lifts your mood and can protect against apathy. You are less likely to postpone tasks, and more likely to take pride in your work or personal projects. Keep in mind that motivation is not always a steady flame; it rises and falls based on many factors, like sleep, stress, and environment. The methods here will help you rediscover motivation when it wanes and maintain it longer during good times.

15.1 Understanding Motivation Blocks

Before diving into ways to boost motivation, it helps to look at what holds it back. Recognizing these barriers can prevent frustration:

1. **Unclear Purpose**: When you are not sure why you are doing something, the effort can feel pointless.
2. **Overwhelm**: Facing a huge project or too many duties at once can lead to paralysis.
3. **Fear of Failure**: Worrying about mistakes can keep you from taking the first step.
4. **Lack of Energy**: If you are tired from lack of sleep or poor nutrition, it is hard to feel driven.
5. **External Expectations**: Trying to live up to someone else's ideals can sap real passion.

By identifying which of these blocks might be affecting you, you can choose the best strategy to address them. For instance, if you realize you are afraid of messing up, you can work on adopting a more flexible viewpoint about mistakes, or create a safer environment to try things in smaller steps.

15.2 Linking Activities to Deeper Values

It is easier to stay motivated when you believe an activity fits something you genuinely care about. If you see your daily tasks as minor or unimportant, interest fades. However, if you connect them to a larger plan, you may feel more eager to press on. For example, if you value learning, then even seemingly small chores—like reading up on a new business approach—can be linked to that larger interest in acquiring knowledge.

- **Identify Core Values**: Examples might include personal growth, security for your family, creative expression, or contributing to the community.
- **Match Tasks to Values**: If you have to finish a report at work, remind yourself that doing this well might open doors for you or your family. Even if the task itself is boring, the bigger outcome holds meaning.
- **Create a Personal Statement**: A short sentence that reminds you why you do what you do: "I push forward in my career to give my kids a stable life," or "I learn new skills to feel more competent and explore fresh possibilities."

By attaching tasks to values, you turn them into stepping stones toward something that resonates with you.

15.3 Daily Goals and "Wins"

One reason people lose motivation is feeling like they make no progress. Large goals can take months or years, so in the short term, it seems like nothing is happening. Counter this by setting small daily targets or tasks you can definitely achieve.

1. **Keep It Simple**: A daily goal might be as modest as making a 30-minute workout happen, spending 10 minutes reading a new book, or doing a quick household task.

2. **Track Wins**: A "win" is any completed task or sign of progress. Write these down somewhere. Seeing a list of completed tasks can give you a boost, especially when your larger project is still in progress.
3. **Celebrate Mentally**: You do not need to throw a party. Just pause and say, "Yes, I did that," acknowledging yourself.
4. **Adjust as Needed**: If you find your daily goals are too easy or too hard, tweak them. The key is to keep them in a range where you feel challenged but not overwhelmed.

Watching these little wins add up day by day can feed your motivation in a real and visible way, rather than relying on a distant outcome alone.

15.4 The Power of Visual Reminders

Some men are very visual learners. Having clear and frequent reminders of what you aim for can spark motivation in moments when you are tempted to slack. You can:

- **Create a Board or Collage**: Gather pictures, phrases, or symbols that represent your goal—whether it is improved health, financial security, or learning a new instrument. Hang this in a place you see daily.
- **Use Phone or Laptop Backgrounds**: Choose an image related to your objective. Each time you check your phone, you see a nudge to stay on track.
- **Sticky Notes**: Post short phrases on your bathroom mirror or near your desk. For instance, "Stay consistent" or "Remember your reason."
- **Audio Cues**: If you prefer audio, set an alarm with a short motivational message or piece of music that energizes you.

These small nudges keep your goal present in your mind, reducing the chance of forgetting or losing focus amid daily distractions.

15.5 Building a Personal Encouragement System

One method to sustain motivation is to create your own "support team" or encouragement system. This goes beyond just telling a friend about your plan—it involves structured contact with people who back you up.

- **Accountability Partner**: Team up with someone who also has goals. Schedule regular check-ins by text, phone, or in-person. Share challenges, progress, and next actions.
- **Group Settings**: This could be a local club, a forum, or even a chat group of individuals working on similar projects or habits. Everyone roots for each other.
- **Mentors or Role Models**: Seek out individuals who have achieved what you are aiming for or who show strong discipline. Ask them for advice or simply watch how they handle setbacks.
- **Close Allies**: Family members or friends can offer consistent reminders of your aims. They can also provide honest feedback if they see you slipping.

Having someone ask, "How is your progress going?" can push you to keep taking steps forward even when you feel less motivated.

15.6 Managing Distractions and Temptations

Modern life is full of potential distractions—social media, streaming platforms, games, and so on. These can drain your time and energy, leaving you too worn out to work on important goals.

1. **Set Rules for Technology**: Restrict certain apps or sites during work hours. Some apps block time-wasting websites for designated periods.
2. **Create a Focused Space**: If possible, have a corner of your home or office free of TV or other interruptions. Keep your phone out of reach, or at least on silent, when you need to concentrate.
3. **Plan Fun Time**: If you enjoy gaming or socializing online, schedule it for after you complete your essential tasks. This approach turns it into a reward rather than a continuous temptation.
4. **Recognize Trigger Points**: Maybe you scroll social media when you are bored. Find a replacement activity—like taking a brief walk or doing some stretches.

Reducing distractions ensures your limited energy is directed to tasks that align with your goals, which in turn supports motivation since you see more results.

15.7 Overcoming Slumps and Ruts

Even with the best plan, you may wake up some days lacking any drive. This does not mean you are doomed; it is a normal fluctuation. Here are ways to push through:

- **Short Burst Method**: Start with just 5 or 10 minutes of the task. Often, beginning is the hardest part. Once you start, momentum can carry you further.
- **Change Location or Method**: If working at home is uninspiring, go to a library or a cafe for a change of scenery. If you are stuck in the same exercise routine, try a different workout.
- **Review Achievements**: Look at your "win list" or think about what you have already accomplished. Remind yourself that you are capable and that one off-day does not erase past progress.
- **Physical Movement**: A quick walk, some push-ups, or a brief yoga session can re-energize the body, which can also clear mental blocks.

Slumps are temporary. By using these small tricks, you can often flip your mindset from "not feeling it today" to "maybe I can do something small right now."

15.8 Internal vs. External Motivation

Motivation can be described as coming from within (internal) or from outside (external). Internal motivation happens when you do an activity because you find it fulfilling or interesting in itself. External motivation might be driven by prizes, money, or recognition from others. Both can be useful, but focusing too much on external perks can be risky. Once the external reward goes away, so might your drive.

- **Explore Your Enjoyment**: Ask yourself if there is any part of the task you like or find interesting. You might discover aspects that spark curiosity or pride.
- **Use External Rewards Wisely**: It is okay to offer yourself a small treat after reaching milestones, but do not rely solely on that.
- **Combine Both**: Perhaps you love the sense of growth that comes from learning a skill (internal) but also appreciate how it might lead to a raise

(external). Recognize both, but nurture the inner satisfaction to keep you going long term.

Understanding where your motivation comes from can help you adjust. If you realize you are only motivated by outside approval, you might try to cultivate a deeper sense of personal satisfaction.

15.9 Visualizing the Finished Task

A simple technique is to picture yourself completing the activity or reaching the goal. This mental image can trigger positive feelings that make you more likely to start working. For instance, if your goal is to finish a big project at work, spend a minute imagining how it will feel to submit it on time and see the positive response from others.

- **Make It Detailed**: Close your eyes and picture the colors, sounds, and setting of completion. Imagine your own emotions—relief, pride, excitement.
- **Keep It Brief**: A short visualization, maybe 30 seconds to a minute, is enough. Doing this too long can become an excuse to avoid actual work.
- **Pair It with Action**: Right after visualizing, do a small related task. This pairs the positive mental image with real forward movement.

While it may feel awkward at first, visualization can reorient your mind toward the payoff, improving your willingness to tackle the work.

15.10 The Role of Habits in Sustaining Motivation

Motivation can be fragile if you rely solely on emotions. Habits, however, create automatic routines that keep you moving even on low-motivation days. Once a habit is set, you do the action without constant internal debate.

- **Pick One Routine at a Time**: Instead of trying to overhaul everything, focus on a single behavior. For example, commit to walking 20 minutes after dinner each day.

- **Use "Triggers"**: Link the habit to something you already do—like after you brush your teeth, you stretch for five minutes. This helps anchor the new habit in your existing schedule.
- **Reward the Habit**: Give yourself a small positive response (even if it is just a mental "good job") immediately after completing the habit.
- **Stay Consistent**: The key to habit formation is repetition. Even if you do it in a short or simplified way, try not to skip days while building it.

Over time, these habits reduce your reliance on feeling "in the mood" or "inspired." You act because it has become part of your routine.

15.11 Using Milestones to Maintain Momentum

When a goal is large or long-term—like earning a degree or losing a significant amount of weight—motivation can fade as the weeks and months pass. Milestones act as checkpoints to see how far you have come and how far you need to go.

1. **Set Several Stages**: Break the big goal into phases with clear numbers or time frames. For instance, if you want to lose 30 pounds, mark every 5 pounds as a milestone.
2. **Create Minor Celebrations**: When you hit a milestone, mark it in your tracker or treat yourself to something modest (like a new book or some quiet time with a friend).
3. **Review What Worked**: After each milestone, note which tactics or behaviors helped you succeed. Keep doing those.
4. **Plan for the Next Step**: Once you celebrate a milestone, quickly set your sights on the next. This prevents you from losing focus after a victory.

By seeing progress in chunks, you avoid being overwhelmed by the entire journey. You also get more frequent opportunities to reaffirm your commitment.

15.12 Staying Motivated in Group or Team Environments

Sometimes you are not the only person with a stake in your goal. Perhaps you work on a group project or share a home renovation plan with a partner. Group motivation can be tricky because you have different personalities and levels of enthusiasm.

- **Set Shared Goals Clearly**: Make sure everyone agrees on the final objective and the smaller steps. This prevents confusion about where you are heading.
- **Divide Duties**: Each member should have a role that fits their strengths, so they feel useful and interested.
- **Hold Regular Check-Ins**: Have brief meetings or updates to see how each person is doing. This keeps people from drifting off-track.
- **Encourage One Another**: Share small wins, give compliments, and suggest help if someone is lagging. Positive group energy can be a strong motivator.

When everyone in the team feels responsible and appreciated, group motivation tends to stay higher.

15.13 Re-evaluating and Recharging

There are times when your motivation dries up, not because you are lazy, but because your life situation or objectives have shifted. It is important to re-evaluate:

- **Check if the Goal Still Fits**: Perhaps your target no longer matches your priorities. Trying to force outdated goals can lead to frustration.
- **Look at Your Current Energy Levels**: Maybe you are dealing with personal stress or health issues. Consider a temporary slowdown or smaller steps until you are back on your feet.
- **Adjust Time Frames**: If your initial timeline is unrealistic, modify it rather than quitting. A flexible timeline can relieve some pressure and renew motivation.
- **Experiment with New Approaches**: If you have lost interest in your routine, try a fresh method, tool, or environment to do the work.

It is not failure to change direction or lighten your load. Sometimes, a short pause or a revised path is the best way to restore motivation.

15.14 Self-Talk and Encouraging Language

Negative self-talk—like calling yourself lazy or a failure—can crush motivation. Changing how you talk to yourself can shift your mindset and keep you engaged:

1. **Use Balanced Phrases**: Instead of "I must do everything perfectly," try "I will do my best today and learn from any mistakes."
2. **Acknowledge Effort**: Praise yourself for showing up, even if the outcome was not 100% perfect.
3. **Avoid Absolutes**: Words like "always" or "never" can lead to drama in your inner monologue. So, avoid "I always fail" or "I never finish anything."
4. **Focus on Solutions**: Replace "I cannot handle this" with "I might need a new approach or extra help."

Over time, supportive inner language fosters a mental environment where motivation can thrive.

15.15 Stress and Motivation

Stress can be a double-edged sword. A small dose can energize you to meet deadlines, but too much can cause burnout or avoidance. Finding the right balance involves:

- **Mindful Techniques**: Deep breathing, short walks, or pauses during the day can lower stress and keep you mentally fresh.
- **Organized Planning**: When tasks feel scattered, stress builds. Use to-do lists or project boards to see everything clearly.
- **Seek Support**: Talk to someone about work or personal stress. Even just venting can help you refocus.
- **Watch for Overload**: If your body or mind is showing signs of exhaustion—frequent headaches, irritation, poor sleep—adjust your workload or timeline.

By managing stress, you protect your motivation. Otherwise, chronic tension can wear you down until you lose your drive completely.

15.16 Learning from Others' Success

One way to spark motivation is to learn from real-world examples. Read biographies, watch interviews, or listen to podcasts of people who have succeeded in the area you are interested in. Notice how they dealt with setbacks or found creative workarounds. This can offer fresh ideas and remind you that obstacles are normal.

- **Pick a Mentor**: If possible, reach out to someone who has done what you want to do. Ask if you can talk or email questions occasionally.
- **Join Discussions**: Online groups or local meetups let you share experiences with peers also trying to achieve something. Everyone can benefit from each other's methods and lessons.
- **Keep an Open Mind**: Do not dismiss someone's experience just because they seem different. You may find a universal takeaway you can adapt to your own life.

Seeing how others overcame similar hurdles can be a strong motivator, showing that your target is achievable.

15.17 Healthy Rewards

Using rewards can be effective, but be mindful of what you choose. If your objective is to improve health, rewarding yourself with large amounts of junk food might send mixed signals. Instead, pick rewards that align with your values or at least do not undermine your progress.

- **Lifestyle-Boosting Rewards**: Buying a quality item for your hobby, investing in comfortable workout clothes, or upgrading something in your work area.
- **Relaxation Rewards**: A calm evening with a good book, a bubble bath, or a gentle stroll outside.
- **Social Rewards**: Spend time with a friend or join a social activity you enjoy. This can double as fun and emotional support.

Attaching these small or medium-sized benefits to milestones can keep you engaged without derailing your main goal.

15.18 Planning for Busy or Hard Times

Sometimes your schedule gets packed or life throws unexpected twists your way—illness, urgent travel, or major changes at work. Motivation can wither if you feel you cannot maintain your usual routines. Anticipate tough periods by creating a "scaled down" version of your plan:

1. **Minimum Action**: Decide on the smallest activity that keeps you connected to your goal, like five minutes of exercise if you cannot do a full workout.
2. **Focus on Key Tasks**: If you only have limited mental energy, prioritize essential duties that move the project forward.
3. **Set Realistic Expectations**: Accept that your pace might slow temporarily. Giving yourself grace can prevent guilt or discouragement.
4. **Resume Full Speed Later**: Once life calms down, ramp back up to your regular plan.

Flexibility in how you approach your goals during hectic times can save your motivation from collapsing altogether.

15.19 Tracking Progress Over Time

Keeping track of improvements not just daily, but monthly or quarterly, can show you the bigger picture. Men sometimes fail to notice how far they have come because they focus on daily ups and downs.

- **Data Logs**: If your goal is financial, maintain a log of your savings or debt reduction. If it is fitness-related, track changes in performance or measurements.
- **Periodic Reviews**: Every month or quarter, spend some time looking at these numbers. Notice trends and adjust accordingly.
- **Reflect on How You Feel**: Progress is not just about numbers. You might have more confidence or less stress. Note these improvements too, as they can motivate you more than raw data.
- **Set New Targets**: Once you meet a certain level, you can create an updated goal to keep the spark alive.

Looking at proof of long-term success is reassuring, especially when your short-term progress might feel slow on certain days.

15.20 Conclusion of Chapter 15

Motivation is not a mystery reserved for a few "high-powered" individuals. It is a mix of clear objectives, personal interest, supportive systems, and daily habits. By linking tasks to your values, setting manageable goals, finding accountability, and tweaking your environment to reduce distractions, you can strengthen your drive. When motivation dips, you can draw on visualization, short bursts of effort, or a support network to get back on track.

Remember that it is normal to feel less motivated on some days. The point is to cultivate strategies that keep you moving forward despite these dips. With time, your success will not hinge on a fleeting burst of inspiration, but rather on a structured plan and consistent follow-through. Our next chapter, Chapter 16, will focus on handling stress in a safe way, which ties closely to motivation. When you learn to manage stress, you preserve the energy and clarity needed to keep your drive alive and your goals within reach.

CHAPTER 16

Handling Stress Without Harm

Introduction
Stress is a natural reaction to demands or challenges, often prompting you to become more alert or take action. However, when stress lasts too long or becomes too intense, it can harm both your body and mind. Men, in particular, can feel pressure to "handle it all" without showing strain, leading to bottled-up anxiety that can burst out in anger or health problems.

This chapter explores different forms of stress, signs that stress is becoming a problem, and methods for handling it safely. We will cover everyday tips like healthy daily habits, as well as ways to manage sudden spikes in tension. You will learn how to recognize stressors, plan realistic coping strategies, and build resilience so that you can handle challenges without damaging your physical or mental well-being. By the end, you will have a clearer idea of how to face life's pressures in a constructive way.

16.1 What Causes Stress?

Stress can come from various sources, which differ from one man to another. Some common examples include:

- **Work Demands**: Tight deadlines, conflicts with colleagues, or feeling stuck in a non-rewarding job.
- **Family Responsibilities**: Financial obligations, caring for children or aging parents, or relationship strife.
- **Major Life Changes**: Relocation, divorce, job loss, or the arrival of a new child can disrupt routines.
- **Social Pressures**: Striving to keep up with peers, meet cultural standards, or feeling judged by relatives.
- **Internal Tensions**: Personal doubts, perfectionist tendencies, or fear of not meeting high expectations.

You may face a mix of these factors at once, which can amplify the pressure. Recognizing your main stressors is a key first step in creating a plan to address them.

16.2 Signs You Are Overstressed

Men sometimes try to push through stress without acknowledging its effects, but certain clues can hint at a brewing problem. If you ignore these indicators, stress can worsen and lead to serious issues. Watch for:

1. **Ongoing Tiredness**: Feeling drained even after you rest.
2. **Physical Ailments**: Frequent headaches, muscle tension, stomach problems, or changes in appetite.
3. **Mood Swings**: Sudden irritability, anger, or anxiety over minor triggers.
4. **Sleep Disturbances**: Trouble falling asleep, waking up in the middle of the night, or feeling unrested in the morning.
5. **Constant Worry**: Thoughts racing, unable to relax or enjoy free time.
6. **Avoidance**: Procrastinating on tasks, skipping work, or dodging social events because you feel overwhelmed.

If these patterns persist, it is time to address your stress levels rather than hope they will disappear on their own.

16.3 Immediate Stress-Reduction Methods

When you sense stress building in real-time—like during a heated meeting or right before a nerve-racking appointment—use short, immediate techniques to calm your body and mind. These can prevent the situation from getting worse.

- **Deep Breathing**: Inhale slowly for a count of four, hold for four, then exhale for four. Repeat several times. This can lower your heart rate and release tension.
- **Muscle Relaxation**: Tighten a specific muscle group (like shoulders or fists) for a few seconds, then let go. Move through different parts of your body.
- **Grounding**: If you feel overwhelmed, focus on something in your environment—like the texture of your desk or the sounds around you. This brings your attention to the present.
- **Take a Short Break**: Even a quick walk or standing outside for a minute can interrupt a stress spiral. Use this pause to regain composure.

These methods help you handle stress in the moment, especially in public or high-pressure settings where you cannot completely withdraw.

16.4 Longer-Term Stress Management Techniques

Beyond handling stress on the spot, developing daily or weekly routines can lower your overall stress load. This helps prevent a chronic cycle of tension that hurts your health.

1. **Regular Exercise**: Physical activity reduces stress hormones and releases beneficial chemicals in the body. It also channels your energy and frustration into movement.
2. **Healthy Diet**: Too much sugar or processed food can destabilize your energy and mood. Including fruits, vegetables, and proteins can keep you more balanced.
3. **Adequate Sleep**: Without enough rest, you become more reactive to stress. Aiming for 7-8 hours per night can strengthen your emotional resilience.
4. **Relaxation Practices**: Activities like gentle stretching, mindfulness, or a hobby that calms you (like painting or fishing) can replenish your mental reserves.
5. **Nature Time**: Spending time outdoors, even if just a short walk in a park, can calm nerves and refresh the mind.

Consistency is crucial. Doing these activities once may help a little, but making them part of your lifestyle can significantly lower chronic stress.

16.5 Setting Realistic Expectations and Boundaries

A major source of stress is trying to do too much or meet everyone's demands without considering your own limits. Learning when to say "no" or adjust your workload can provide breathing room.

- **Clarify Work Duties**: Talk with supervisors or teammates if tasks are unclear or too heavy. A short conversation can sometimes redistribute responsibilities or adjust deadlines.
- **Limit Commitments**: You do not have to attend every social event or volunteer for all extracurricular activities. Choose what aligns most with your priorities.
- **Protect Personal Time**: Schedule downtime in your calendar just as you would a meeting. During that time, avoid work emails or extra chores if possible.

- **Be Honest**: If you are overwhelmed, let relevant people know. Hiding your stress can worsen it, while being open might lead to practical solutions or help.

By setting limits, you can prevent stress from building to a crisis point. It may feel uncomfortable at first, but healthy boundaries are part of maintaining long-term well-being.

16.6 Communication Skills for Stress Reduction

Referring back to earlier chapters on communication: how you express needs and handle conflict can either raise or lower your stress. Misunderstandings or unspoken resentments often fuel tension.

- **Speak Up Early**: If a coworker or family member is causing you extra pressure, bring it up calmly before frustration boils over.
- **Use "I" Statements**: Instead of accusing them—"You always burden me"—try "I feel overwhelmed when tasks pile up suddenly."
- **Negotiate Solutions**: Work together to see if tasks can be shifted or if more support can be provided.
- **Ask Questions**: If you are unclear about someone's expectations, ask for details so you are not stressing about unknown requirements.

Effective communication can resolve small problems before they turn into large stressors.

16.7 Identifying Stress "Triggers"

In addition to broad sources of stress like work or family, there can be specific triggers that spike your tension. These might be words people say, certain times of day, or particular tasks you dislike.

- **Keep a Stress Log**: When you notice tension rising, jot down what was happening. Over time, patterns may emerge—like a certain coworker's behavior or tasks that involve public speaking.
- **Plan Coping Responses**: If you know you have to do a stressful task, schedule a break afterward or have a friend lined up to talk with.

- **Reframe the Trigger**: Sometimes changing how you view the situation helps. Instead of dreading a budget meeting, see it as a chance to provide valuable input.
- **Discuss with Others**: If the same triggers keep popping up, share them with a trusted person. They might offer tips on how they handle similar stressors.

By pinpointing triggers, you can prepare or avoid them rather than being caught off guard each time.

16.8 The Mind-Body Connection

Stress is not just mental; it affects your body in ways like raised blood pressure, muscle tightness, and increased cortisol levels. Likewise, caring for your body helps shield your mind from excess stress.

1. **Stretching and Movement**: Regularly moving your neck, shoulders, and back reduces the muscle tension that often builds up under stress.
2. **Progressive Muscle Relaxation**: Tense each muscle group (feet, legs, abdomen, etc.) and release. This practice can lower overall tension and help you recognize when your body is bracing itself.
3. **Breathing Exercises**: Proper oxygen flow calms the nervous system. You can do belly breathing, counting your breaths, or other variations.
4. **Physical Hobbies**: Sports, dancing, or even gardening can provide an outlet for pent-up energy. The goal is not to become the best, but to find a physically engaging activity that you enjoy.

By tending to your body, you create a shield against the toll that stress tries to take on your well-being.

16.9 Avoiding Harmful Coping Methods

Under severe stress, some men turn to alcohol, overeating, gambling, or other risky behaviors as a form of escape. While these might offer temporary relief, they often create bigger problems down the line.

- **Recognize Warning Signs**: If you find yourself relying on substances or activities that harm you financially, physically, or emotionally, step back and evaluate.
- **Seek Professional Help**: A counselor or support group can guide you if you feel dependent on damaging habits. This is not weakness; it is a step toward healthier choices.
- **Replace with Positive Outlets**: Instead of drinking to unwind, consider a calming bath, reading, or playing a casual sport. Identify safe alternatives that give you a break without negative consequences.
- **Share with Allies**: If you have friends or family who can provide support, let them know you are trying to avoid certain destructive patterns.

The key is to treat the root of stress rather than using harmful distractions that only make the situation worse later.

16.10 Time-Out Strategy for Anger

Stress can lead to anger outbursts if not managed. Men sometimes feel pressure to remain stoic, and anger may be the only emotion they allow themselves to show. However, explosive anger can harm relationships and health. The "time-out" method can help:

1. **Notice Rising Anger**: Recognize the physical signs—heart rate speeding up, clenched jaw, or a hot feeling in your face.
2. **Step Away Politely**: Tell the person involved, "I need a minute," and remove yourself from the situation.
3. **Calm Down**: Breathe slowly, splash water on your face, or go for a short walk. Focus on letting the adrenaline decrease.
4. **Return and Discuss**: Once calmer, approach the issue more rationally. This prevents saying or doing things in the heat of the moment that cause regret.

This structured pause can save you from further stress and build healthier communication habits over time.

16.11 Stress and Work-Life Balance

Work can become overwhelming, leaving little room for personal life. Over time, this imbalance can lead to burnout—a state of physical, mental, and emotional exhaustion. To protect against this:

- **Set Work Limits**: If possible, avoid checking work emails after a certain hour or on weekends. This boundary helps you recharge.
- **Prioritize Tasks**: Know which tasks are truly urgent. Sometimes, we put pressure on ourselves to do everything at once.
- **Use Vacation Days**: Men sometimes pride themselves on never taking a break. Regular breaks or time off can actually raise long-term productivity.
- **Communicate with Loved Ones**: If work is very busy, let family or friends know, and plan quality moments when possible. They can be supportive if they understand the situation.

Maintaining a healthy balance ensures you do not become defined solely by your job, which in turn reduces the risk of stress overload.

16.12 Building a Support System

One powerful buffer against stress is having a network of caring people. This could include family, friends, a partner, or colleagues you trust. Sharing burdens can lighten them, both emotionally and practically.

- **Honest Conversations**: Let people know when you are struggling. Sometimes just voicing concerns can bring relief or new ideas.
- **Community Groups**: Joining groups focused on shared interests—like running clubs or hobby circles—can give you a sense of belonging.
- **Professional Support**: Therapists, counselors, or support hotlines exist for those who need structured help, especially if stress is chronic or severe.
- **Give and Take**: Offer support to others when they face stress. Being helpful can also remind you that you are not alone in dealing with life's hurdles.

A solid support system does not solve every problem, but it can make stress more manageable by providing empathy, advice, and sometimes hands-on assistance.

16.13 Simple Mindful Exercises

Stress often arises from replaying past errors or fearing future outcomes. Mindful exercises pull you into the present moment, reducing worry loops.

- **Observing the Senses**: Sit quietly and list five things you can see, four things you can feel, three you can hear, two you can smell, and one you can taste. This grounds you in the now.
- **Breathing Countdown**: Breathe in for a count of five, out for five, then repeat, lowering the count each time. Focus on each number.
- **Body Scan**: Close your eyes and mentally travel from your toes to your head, noticing any tension or sensation. Release tension where you find it.

These quick exercises can be done nearly anywhere, offering immediate relief from a racing mind.

16.14 Taming Perfectionism

Men who strive for perfection in every area may push themselves too hard and constantly feel stressed about meeting sky-high standards. While aiming high can be good, impossible standards create continuous pressure.

- **Set Realistic Goals**: Use the methods discussed in Chapter 13 to ensure your targets are doable.
- **Recognize "Good Enough"**: Some tasks only require a decent job, not absolute perfection. Decide which tasks truly demand top-notch results and which do not.
- **Learn from Errors**: Mistakes are part of the learning process, not proof you are inadequate.
- **Celebrate Small Progress**: Instead of focusing on what is missing, notice what you did well. This shift in mindset lowers stress and boosts drive.

By easing rigid perfectionism, you allow space for steady improvement without the chronic pressure that drains well-being.

16.15 Handling Stress in Public or Work Settings

Sometimes, stress hits when you are in a place where you cannot openly do deep relaxation or fully walk away (like in a meeting or in a public space). You can still manage stress discreetly:

1. **Breathing in Steps**: Inhale deeply and slowly, but quietly. Your coworkers likely will not notice.
2. **Use a Pen and Paper**: Jot down a quick note of your thoughts or what is bothering you. This externalizes worry and can be done secretly in many settings.
3. **Shift Posture**: Roll your shoulders back, sit up straight, and relax your hands. Tension often shows up in hunched shoulders or clenched fists.
4. **Micro-Break**: Excuse yourself to the restroom or get a glass of water. Even one minute away from the scene can help you reset.

These mini-tactics can keep stress from spiraling out of control until you can find a better time and place to handle it fully.

16.16 Recognizing When Professional Help Is Needed

Sometimes stress grows too large to manage alone. It may manifest as chronic anxiety, panic attacks, depression, or serious physical issues. If you have tried healthy coping strategies but still feel overwhelmed, consider:

- **Therapy**: A counselor can offer tools tailored to your personality and situation.
- **Support Groups**: Meeting others who face similar stressors can help you feel less isolated.
- **Medical Checkup**: Stress can affect blood pressure, heart health, and more. A doctor can identify any stress-related issues and suggest steps.
- **Short-Term Medication**: Under a professional's care, medication can sometimes help stabilize acute stress or anxiety.

Seeking help is not giving up. It is making use of resources that can guide you through a heavy challenge.

16.17 Building Resilience for the Future

Resilience is your capacity to bounce back after hardship. By focusing on certain habits and mindsets, you can toughen your response to future stress:

- **Positive View of Challenges**: See hardships as temporary and solvable. This mindset makes you more confident in facing them.
- **Strong Connections**: Keep nurturing close relationships. Having allies at your side boosts resilience.
- **Learning Orientation**: Approach each stressful event as a lesson, analyzing what can be adjusted next time.
- **Balanced Lifestyle**: Keep your basics—sleep, nutrition, exercise—in check. A healthy body and mind are more adaptable.

Over time, each hurdle you overcome contributes to your personal strength, making the next trial less overwhelming.

16.18 Applying Reflection to Stress

Reflection, discussed in Chapter 14, can also reduce stress by encouraging you to examine daily events. By writing or thinking about your frustrations, you can spot unhealthy patterns or triggers more quickly. Reflection helps you separate real problems from imagined ones, so you can direct your energy to genuine issues instead of worrying needlessly. This, in turn, eases stress over things that are not truly within your responsibility or power to change.

16.19 Small Adjustments for Big Results

Sometimes men aim for a complete life overhaul when they feel stressed—quitting a job, moving to another place, or making major changes overnight. While that might occasionally be warranted, small consistent tweaks can also yield big stress relief:

- **Simplify Your Space**: A cluttered home or desk can subconsciously add to stress. Clearing it can create a sense of calm.
- **Plan a Pleasant Activity**: Adding a short walk, 10 minutes of fun reading, or another easy pastime each day can serve as a mental break.
- **Cut Down on Media Overload**: Constant negative news or online drama can raise tension. Limit how frequently you check these.
- **Ask for Help**: If your daily errands are overwhelming, consider delegating certain tasks to a friend or family member, or even hiring help if possible.

By reducing or removing small stressors, you open up more mental space to tackle larger concerns.

16.20 Conclusion of Chapter 16

Stress is part of modern life, but it does not have to dominate you. By understanding the common causes, recognizing the signs, and adopting both quick fixes and long-term habits, men can lower stress to manageable levels. Techniques like mindful breathing, physical activity, and setting boundaries help you cope day to day. Meanwhile, building a supportive network, practicing honest communication, and ensuring healthy routines fortify you against chronic stress.

Not every stress management method will work for every individual, so it is essential to try a few and see which best suits your personality and situation. The key takeaway is that stress does not have to be a silent enemy slowly harming your health and relationships. You can confront it with practical, steady actions. As we move on to Chapters 17 and 18, we will explore how to balance personal needs and relationships, and how to create a reliable support network—both of which connect closely to stress control. A well-managed life, with room for rest and clear boundaries, promotes greater freedom from harmful stress.

CHAPTER 17

Balancing Personal Needs and Relationships

Introduction

Many men try to do well in every area of life—work, family, friendships, personal goals—only to feel pulled in too many directions. Learning to balance personal needs with the demands of relationships can be tricky. Sometimes, men sacrifice their own well-being to keep the peace at home or maintain a certain image at work. Other times, they might swing the other way, becoming so focused on their individual aims that close relationships suffer neglect.

This chapter will explore ways to respect your own limits and wants while also caring for the people around you. We will look at setting boundaries, sharing responsibilities in relationships, and making time for personal growth without shutting out loved ones. By the end, you should have practical steps to pursue your goals and personal well-being while also staying attentive to the bonds that matter most to you.

17.1 Recognizing the Importance of Balance

Relationships bring joy, support, and a sense of belonging. Personal needs—health, leisure, mental well-being—are also essential. If you ignore your own well-being entirely, you risk burnout, resentment, or feeling unfulfilled. If you always put yourself first, you may damage important bonds or become isolated. Balance is key for a life that feels both stable and rewarding.

- **Preventing Burnout**: Without time for yourself, you can become overwhelmed, which can harm not only you but also those who rely on you.
- **Strengthening Bonds**: When you are physically and mentally well, you can show up more fully for the people in your life.
- **Personal Growth**: Having space for your own interests and needs leads to self-discovery and ongoing development, which can also enrich your relationships.

Balancing these elements is not about perfection. It is about avoiding extremes and making daily adjustments so that neither personal needs nor relationships are consistently neglected.

17.2 Setting Boundaries with Loved Ones

Boundaries define what you are comfortable with and what you are not, in terms of time, energy, and personal space. Many men find it difficult to say "no," especially to family or close friends. Yet boundaries are not walls to keep people out; they are guidelines that protect healthy interaction.

1. **Identify Your Limits**: Think about situations that leave you drained or resentful. Are you taking too many phone calls from friends, doing too many favors, or always working overtime for your boss?
2. **Communicate Clearly**: Politely let people know your capacity. For instance, "I am happy to help, but I cannot do it this weekend," or "I need some quiet time tonight."
3. **Be Consistent**: If you bend your boundary every time someone applies pressure, they may assume your limit does not exist.
4. **Recognize Others' Boundaries**: Healthy relationships go both ways. Respect the limits of friends and family as well.

Setting boundaries might cause short-term discomfort, but it often leads to healthier, more respectful interactions in the long run.

17.3 Finding Time for Personal Hobbies and Goals

It is easy to lose yourself in your roles as a partner, parent, or employee. If you never do anything purely for your own interest, life can feel repetitive or empty. Personal hobbies and goals refresh the mind and keep you aware of your individual identity.

- **Schedule It**: Just as you might plan a doctor's appointment or a date, block out a regular time for your own pursuits—whether it is reading, learning a skill, or engaging in a sport.

- **Small Windows Count**: If life is busy, even 15 minutes a day or a couple of short sessions a week can help. A consistent mini-break for a hobby can go a long way.
- **Include Loved Ones**: Sometimes, you can combine personal interests with family or friends. For example, if you enjoy cooking, involve your partner or kids in simple meal prep. If you like walking in nature, invite someone along.
- **Stay Flexible**: Life changes often. You may need to adjust how much time you devote to hobbies during especially busy phases. The key is not to drop them entirely but to adapt.

By giving some attention to personal goals, you maintain a sense of self that does not depend solely on external roles or relationships.

17.4 Balancing Career Ambitions and Home Life

Work can consume a large share of your day. Many men feel pressured to achieve or earn more, fearing that slowing down might harm their professional reputation or paycheck. Yet focusing on your career at the expense of home life can cause tension, loneliness, or a lack of connection with loved ones.

1. **Define Success for Yourself**: Reflect on whether chasing higher status or bigger paychecks is truly your personal definition of success, or if it is coming from others' expectations.
2. **Set Work Boundaries**: If possible, avoid answering work messages late at night. Communicate your preferred times of availability. Let your employer or team know the best ways to contact you for urgent issues, so you do not always feel on call.
3. **Quality Over Quantity**: If your schedule is demanding, plan meaningful activities with family when you can—like a special weekend outing or device-free dinner times. Short, focused bonding can be more valuable than many hours of half-attention.
4. **Use Time Off**: If you have vacation or personal days, take them. Stepping away from work can recharge your energy, making you more effective when you return.

Work-life balance often requires ongoing adjustments, as career demands and personal needs evolve. Staying aware of these shifts helps you prevent burnout or neglect of your family or yourself.

17.5 Practical Ways to Share Responsibilities at Home

In many households, conflicts arise when one person shoulders most chores or family duties. Sharing tasks fairly can ease tension and free each partner to pursue some personal interests.

- **Discuss Expectations**: Sit down and list out daily, weekly, and monthly tasks—like cooking, cleaning, shopping, paying bills. Figure out who does what and whether a rotation makes sense.
- **Play to Strengths**: If you are good at finances, handle the budget. If your partner cooks better, let them handle meals. However, remain open to switching roles to avoid boredom or skill gaps.
- **Use Checklists or Calendars**: A shared digital calendar or a whiteboard can outline responsibilities. This reduces guesswork and arguments over who was supposed to do what.
- **Allow Flexibility**: Unexpected events can occur. Be willing to swap tasks or step in for each other when needed. Grudges can build if one partner is rigid and inflexible.

Working as a team at home lightens the load, lowers conflict, and gives both people more space for personal growth.

17.6 Maintaining Individual Identity in a Committed Relationship

Being a partner in a close relationship does not mean you must lose your uniqueness. Some men feel they have to merge entirely with their partner's interests or social circle, leaving little room for their own. Keeping an individual identity is healthy for both sides.

1. **Nurture Personal Passions**: Continue engaging in hobbies or goals you had before, unless they have ceased to interest you.
2. **Encourage Each Other**: If your partner has a different hobby, show genuine curiosity or support, and expect the same in return.
3. **Have Solo Friendships**: It is good to have shared friends, but also maintain bonds independent of your partner. This provides variety and fresh perspectives.
4. **Speak Up About Your Needs**: If you need some alone time to read or relax, say so. Clear communication is less hurtful than silently pulling away.

Finding the balance between closeness and independence can help your relationship remain lively and prevent resentment.

17.7 Conflict Resolution When Needs Clash

Sometimes your personal need for solitude or self-improvement might clash with family events or your partner's requests. This is normal. The key is respectful resolution that values both sides.

- **Listen First**: Hear why the other person feels their need is urgent. Ask questions to fully understand their perspective.
- **Explain Your Position**: Use calm, clear statements about why you need time for yourself or want to pursue a certain activity.
- **Seek Middle Ground**: Maybe you can postpone your personal task to a different day, or shorten the time so you can also attend a family gathering. Alternatively, the other person may shift their schedule to fit yours.
- **Agree on a Trial**: If you cannot decide on a permanent solution, test one for a week or month. See how it goes, then review and adjust.

Healthy relationships can handle conflicts of interest if both sides are willing to communicate and compromise.

17.8 The Importance of Rest and Recharge

Balancing relationships with personal needs should include rest for the body and mind. Continuous activity—whether it is social events, work, or home duties—burns out even the most energetic men.

- **Plan Recovery Times**: Schedule short breaks or rest days. If you are a busy parent or worker, coordinate these moments with family to ensure you actually get them.
- **Pick Soothing Activities**: Maybe you read, go for a gentle walk, or spend quiet time listening to music. The activity is less important than its calming effect.
- **Watch for Overcommitment**: If you notice your schedule has zero free blocks, it might be time to scale back.

- **Use Bedtime Wisely**: Try to wind down with minimal screen use. Quality sleep is a key recharge factor that affects mood, energy, and how you relate to others.

By carving out time for rest, you stay healthier and more available for quality interactions with the people you care about.

17.9 Checking in with Yourself Regularly

It can be easy to slide into old habits of pleasing everyone else or ignoring your relationships. A quick, regular self-check can reveal if you are leaning too far in one direction.

1. **Weekly Reflection**: Ask yourself how you feel physically and mentally. Are you tense? Exhausted? When was the last time you enjoyed some personal free time?
2. **Assess Relationship Health**: Consider whether loved ones are complaining about your absence, or if you have missed important events. Are your children or partner showing signs of feeling neglected?
3. **Adjust as Needed**: If you find a clear imbalance—too much focus on personal projects or too little personal space—make a plan to correct it.
4. **Involve Others**: If your relationship is very close, talk about these findings together. A supportive partner can offer feedback or ideas on how to shift.

Consistent small corrections keep you from drifting into extremes that lead to frustration and resentment.

17.10 Handling Guilt About Saying "No"

When men are used to being the "go-to" person for favors or help, they might feel guilty if they turn down requests or set personal boundaries. Remember:

- **Guilt Is a Signal, Not a Fact**: Feeling guilty does not always mean you did something wrong. It might just be your brain adjusting to new boundaries.

- **Protect Your Health**: A well-rested, balanced person can help others better over the long run than someone who is consistently drained.
- **Be Polite but Firm**: Saying "no" can be done with kindness: "I wish I could help, but I already have too much on my plate."
- **Offer Alternatives**: If possible, suggest a different person or a later time you might be available. This shows goodwill without overextending yourself.

Over time, the people around you will learn to respect your boundaries, and you will grow more comfortable standing by them.

17.11 Balancing Needs When Caring for Dependents

Caring for children, aging parents, or a spouse with health issues adds another level of challenge. Men in caretaker roles often feel they must always be on duty. Yet ignoring your needs can lead to exhaustion or even resentment.

- **Ask for Help**: Siblings, friends, neighbors, or community services might share the load. Do not assume you must handle everything alone.
- **Schedule Breaks**: Even a few hours away can restore your patience and sanity. If finances allow, consider hiring help for certain tasks.
- **Join Support Groups**: Sharing experiences with others who also care for dependents can help you learn coping methods and reduce isolation.
- **Plan for Emergencies**: Think in advance about back-up plans if your responsibilities become too heavy. This might be a relative or a close friend who can step in occasionally.

Remember that providing care does not mean you must neglect your own health or personal growth.

17.12 Sharing Your Goals with Loved Ones

If you have personal aspirations, telling your partner, close friends, or family about them can make balancing easier. By knowing what drives you, they may be more supportive or willing to help find space in the schedule.

- **Explain Why It Matters**: Let them see how your personal pursuit connects to your overall happiness or a shared future vision, such as improving career prospects for the family.
- **Ask for Input**: They might have ideas on how to fit your goals into busy routines. Or they might volunteer to take on some duties to give you free time.
- **Agree on Boundaries**: For instance, you might devote an hour each evening to study or practice, and then spend the rest of the night with your partner or kids.
- **Show Appreciation**: Acknowledge their support. This can encourage them to stay enthusiastic about your goals.

When loved ones feel included rather than shut out, balancing becomes a joint effort rather than a tug-of-war.

17.13 Respecting a Partner's Independence

Balance is not just about your needs; your partner also has personal goals. Some men feel uneasy if their partner is off doing something separate, but respecting each other's independent interests can make the bond stronger.

- **Encourage Their Hobbies**: If your partner wants to try a new class or go on a trip with friends, show support. This sets a tone of mutual respect for personal growth.
- **Avoid Jealousy**: Understand that having different interests is healthy and does not threaten a stable relationship.
- **Coordinate Schedules**: If both of you have personal hobbies, coordinate so family responsibilities are covered.
- **Stay Interested**: Ask your partner about what they are learning or experiencing. They will likely return the favor, showing enthusiasm for your projects as well.

A relationship that allows both people room to explore can stay fresh and free from built-up frustration.

17.14 Building Skills for Adaptability

Balancing personal needs and relationships is not a static state—you will have to adjust as life changes. Being adaptable can keep both your well-being and your relationships stable.

- **Stay Open to Feedback**: If a loved one says you have been absent too much, try not to become defensive. Consider their perspective and see if there is a fair point.
- **Reassess Goals**: Life events—like a new job, a move, or a health challenge—may require changing how much time you put into personal projects or social activities.
- **Short-Term vs. Long-Term**: If a project at work is urgent, you might temporarily reduce hobby time. But plan to restore it when the crunch ends.
- **Keep Communicating**: Let people know if you anticipate a busy period or if you want to shift your focus. Clarity prevents misunderstandings.

This flexibility helps you maintain equilibrium even when external conditions shift dramatically.

17.15 Avoiding Extreme Self-Sacrifice

Some men take pride in always putting others first, but extreme sacrifice can cause mental or physical harm. You cannot pour from an empty cup. Finding a balance ensures you can continue to support loved ones for years to come.

- **Check for Resentment**: Do you secretly feel annoyed that you are always helping but not receiving enough back? This can signal an unbalanced situation.
- **Practice Self-Kindness**: Recognize when you do something for yourself without guilt. This is not selfishness; it is self-care.
- **Teach Loved Ones to Cope**: If you do every chore, other family members may not learn or do their part. Over-functioning can create dependency.
- **Seek Fairness**: A good relationship is not about everyone doing exactly the same tasks, but about making sure no one person is severely overburdened all the time.

While generosity is admirable, ensure it does not come at the cost of your health or emotional stability.

17.16 Using Joint Activities to Grow Together

Balancing personal needs with relationships also means finding ways to merge both. Rather than seeing them as separate, you can look for joint activities that satisfy your interests and help you bond.

- **Shared Exercise**: Going for a run or doing a quick workout with your partner can check both "fitness" and "quality time" boxes.
- **Creative Projects**: If you enjoy a certain craft or DIY activity, invite your family to participate. This can teach them new skills while giving you togetherness.
- **Date Nights with a Twist**: Instead of the usual dinner, sign up for a fun class or workshop that interests both of you.
- **Weekend Outings**: Plan brief trips that incorporate something each person loves—such as a short hike for you and a local museum for your partner.

These blended experiences allow you to nurture personal passions and maintain a strong connection at the same time.

17.17 Recognizing When Professional Guidance May Help

If attempts to balance personal needs and relationships lead to frequent fights, emotional distance, or severe stress, it might be time to seek professional help. A counselor, therapist, or life coach can provide strategies tailored to your situation.

- **Relationship Counseling**: If repeated conflicts revolve around who does what or how much time each person gets alone, couples therapy can help clarify roles and expectations.
- **Individual Therapy**: Sometimes, men carry deep patterns—like fear of disappointing others or being overly controlling. Therapy can address these roots, making balance easier.

- **Workplace Coaching**: If your main struggle is managing career demands without harming personal life, a career coach may offer practical scheduling and communication tips.
- **Online or Group Sessions**: If in-person sessions are difficult, online options or local support groups can still provide fresh viewpoints.

Professional insights can often break unhelpful cycles and lead to lasting improvements in how you handle both personal desires and shared commitments.

17.18 Being Present in Relationships

Balancing is not just about time allocation but also about quality of presence. You can spend hours with family but still be mentally checked out, scrolling on your phone or worrying about work. Aim to be truly there when you are with people.

- **Limit Device Use**: Put the phone on silent during meals or shared activities. This small habit can drastically improve interaction.
- **Listen Actively**: When loved ones speak, give them your full attention—eye contact, nodding, asking clarifying questions.
- **Plan Engaging Moments**: Sometimes it helps to plan fun or meaningful activities, rather than passively watching TV.
- **Show Gratitude**: Whether it is a kind word or a small gesture, letting people know you appreciate them adds warmth to the relationship.

Balancing personal needs with relationships is not just about dividing the pie of time. It is also about being fully involved in each moment you dedicate to others.

17.19 Celebrating Milestones Together

Even though you avoid certain words, we can still note the importance of marking achievements or special moments. Sharing successes—yours or your loved ones'—creates stronger connections and reminds everyone that support goes both ways. If you hit a personal fitness goal, let your partner or friends know. If your child finishes a tough project, join in commending their effort. This fosters a sense that your progress is linked to the well-being of the entire household, making balance feel rewarding rather than isolating.

17.20 Conclusion of Chapter 17

Balancing personal needs and relationships is a lifelong process of slight course corrections. You do not have to choose between being completely selfless or entirely self-focused. By setting boundaries, sharing duties, communicating openly, and making room for your own well-being, you can maintain a stable middle ground. Personal health and strong relationships are not enemies—they can enrich each other when approached wisely.

This approach calls for awareness, honest conversation, and a willingness to adapt as life changes. Whether it is negotiating tasks at home, carving out small pockets of time for a hobby, or learning to say "no" politely, each small action can lead to a more fulfilling life. In the next chapter, we will explore how to create a dependable support network (Chapter 18). That topic goes hand in hand with balancing personal needs, because having people you trust makes it easier to manage life's demands without sacrificing your own well-being.

CHAPTER 18

Creating a Support Network

Introduction

No man is an island. While independence is valuable, a personal support network can offer stability during hard times and fresh perspectives when you face challenges. Unfortunately, many men shy away from asking for help or sharing vulnerable feelings, believing they must handle problems alone. As a result, they miss out on the strength and comfort that a supportive circle can provide.

In this chapter, we will discuss the value of having various types of supportive contacts—friends, mentors, professional helpers, and community groups—and how to build and maintain these bonds. We will also look at how to reciprocate, offering support to others in turn. By the end, you should see that forming a reliable network is not a sign of weakness; it is a wise step that can improve mental health, job success, and overall life satisfaction.

18.1 Understanding What a Support Network Is

A support network is simply a group of people or resources you can lean on, learn from, or trust. It can include:

- **Close Friends**: Those who listen without judgment, give honest feedback, and help you unwind.
- **Family Members**: Siblings, parents, or extended relatives who offer practical help or emotional grounding.
- **Mentors or Role Models**: People who have walked a path similar to yours (in career, personal goals, or life philosophy) and can share wisdom.
- **Professional Support**: Therapists, counselors, coaches, or specialized advisors.
- **Community or Faith Groups**: Neighbors, clubs, volunteer organizations, and other group settings where you can form bonds.

This network does not have to be huge. Even a few reliable connections can make a world of difference.

18.2 Why Men Often Lack Strong Support

There are various reasons why some men end up with weak or minimal networks:

1. **Cultural Pressure**: Some societies teach men that asking for help is "soft" or not masculine.
2. **Busy Schedules**: Juggling work and family can leave little time for cultivating friendships.
3. **Fear of Judgement**: Worrying that others might see them as weak or incompetent if they open up.
4. **Past Experiences**: Men who have been let down or betrayed by friends or relatives may find it hard to trust.

Recognizing these barriers is the first step to moving past them. You can then learn to build and maintain supportive ties without feeling embarrassed or overly exposed.

18.3 Starting with One-to-One Friendships

For many men, the easiest place to begin is with a single friend or acquaintance. Building a trusting bond does not require a large group; you just need one person you can reach out to.

- **Reconnect with Old Friends**: Sometimes life pulls friends apart. A simple call or message can reopen lines of communication.
- **Bond over Common Interests**: If you meet someone at a local workshop, gym, or social event, invite them for coffee or to practice the activity together. Friendship often begins with shared enjoyment.
- **Show Genuine Interest**: Ask about their life, goals, or challenges. Listening attentively can deepen a connection.
- **Offer Your Support**: Friendships grow when both parties feel cared about. If your new friend is dealing with a problem, see if there is a small way you can assist.

Over time, these individual connections can form the foundation of a broader network.

18.4 Joining Groups and Clubs

A practical way to meet supportive people is to become part of an existing community. This can feel more natural than cold-approaching strangers, because you already share a common focus. Examples include:

- **Sports Teams or Fitness Classes**: Recreation leagues, martial arts dojos, or running clubs can foster camaraderie.
- **Hobby Circles**: Car restoration groups, cooking classes, board game clubs—whatever interests you, there is likely a meetup.
- **Professional Associations**: Industry groups or local business gatherings can help you find mentors or peers who understand your career path.
- **Volunteer Organizations**: Serving the community alongside others can form strong friendships based on shared passion for a cause.

When you see the same people regularly, deeper bonds can develop more quickly.

18.5 Finding or Becoming a Mentor

Mentors are individuals who guide you based on their experiences. They might offer career advice, life lessons, or emotional support. Finding a mentor does not require an official program; sometimes it grows naturally out of a friendship or work relationship.

- **Identify Potential Mentors**: Look for people who have skills or qualities you admire. They do not have to be older—just more experienced in the area that interests you.
- **Ask Politely**: If you have a rapport, you can request occasional coffee chats or advice sessions. Many successful people enjoy passing on their knowledge.
- **Stay Respectful**: Keep track of what you ask. Mentors are busy and want to see you apply their advice, not waste time.
- **Return the Favor**: You might mentor someone else in an area where you have expertise. Offering guidance can also sharpen your own understanding.

Mentor-mentee relationships can be powerful, providing both direction and a sense of belonging.

18.6 Leaning on Professional Help

Sometimes problems require deeper knowledge than friends or mentors can provide, such as mental health issues, career re-direction, or complex personal crises. Professional help can be a pillar of your support network:

- **Therapists or Counselors**: They are trained to handle emotional and behavioral patterns, offering coping strategies.
- **Career Coaches**: If you feel stuck in your job path, a coach can give structured assessments and help you explore new options.
- **Financial Advisors**: Money stress is common. A reliable advisor can help you organize finances, reduce debt, and plan for the future.
- **Health Specialists**: For ongoing stress or physical concerns, medical professionals and wellness coaches can keep you on track.

Seeking professional help is a responsible move, not a weakness. Think of them as experts you pay to fix or tune up important aspects of your life, much like you would hire a mechanic for your car.

18.7 Building Trust with Others

Trust does not appear instantly. It emerges when both sides consistently behave with honesty, respect, and understanding. To foster trust:

1. **Share Gradually**: Start by sharing small personal details or asking for minor favors. As positive experiences stack up, you can open up more.
2. **Honor Confidentiality**: If a friend shares something private, keep it to yourself unless they say otherwise.
3. **Show Up in Times of Need**: Loyalty during someone's tough moments cements a bond more than casual chats.
4. **Admit Mistakes**: If you slip up or forget an important detail, apologize sincerely. This transparency encourages the other person to be open too.

Trust-building is a mutual process, requiring both parties to invest time and caring attention.

18.8 Developing Emotional Openness

One reason men's networks sometimes lack depth is that emotional openness is discouraged in certain social circles. To get genuine support, you need to feel safe sharing difficulties, not just surface-level chat about sports or work.

- **Find Supportive Listeners**: Notice who genuinely listens without trying to overshadow you with their own stories.
- **Practice Gradual Disclosure**: Start with something slightly more personal than usual. If they respond well, keep going step by step.
- **Drop the Act**: Try not to feel pressured into always appearing strong or in control. Being real about doubts or fears can deepen a bond.
- **Encourage Others**: Show that you can handle their truths without mocking or trivializing them. Emotional openness grows when it is mutual.

This does not mean sharing every detail of your life. It means allowing some real vulnerability to create honest connections.

18.9 How to Give Support in Return

A network is a two-way street. If you only take from others, your bonds may weaken over time. Learn how to give support as well:

- **Active Listening**: Let them finish their thoughts without interruption. Use small confirmations like "I see" or "That must be hard."
- **Ask Thoughtful Questions**: This shows genuine interest and can help them find clarity.
- **Offer Help Within Reason**: Whether it is a ride to the airport or an introduction to someone in your field, small acts of kindness build goodwill.
- **Stay Reliable**: If you promise something, do it. Reliability cements trust and respect.

When both sides of the connection feel supported, the bond becomes robust and enduring.

18.10 Community Resources and Clubs

Beyond personal friends or mentors, community organizations often exist to help men in different aspects of life:

- **Support Groups**: Whether for single fathers, veterans, or men facing certain health issues, these groups provide an environment where members understand your struggles.
- **Local Nonprofits**: Some nonprofits offer job training, mental health services, or social gatherings aimed at men's well-being.
- **Public Classes**: Workshops at community centers or libraries can be low-cost (or free) ways to learn new skills while meeting like-minded people.
- **Online Platforms**: If you live in a remote area or have a busy schedule, online groups can be a lifeline, though they lack the full personal touch of in-person contact.

By mixing community resources with personal connections, you create a wider safety net.

18.11 Handling Disappointments in Relationships

Not every potential friend or mentor will be trustworthy, and sometimes people let each other down. Disappointments are part of human interaction, but they do not have to stop you from seeking support.

1. **Acknowledge Feelings**: It is natural to feel hurt or angry if someone betrays you or fails to help when promised.
2. **Address Issues Directly**: If feasible, calmly share how their behavior affected you. Sometimes a misunderstanding can be repaired through open conversation.
3. **Weigh Future Trust**: If someone repeatedly breaks promises, you might limit the closeness of that bond.
4. **Avoid Overgeneralizing**: One or two bad experiences do not mean all people are untrustworthy.

Learning to navigate letdowns helps you maintain a healthy network by focusing on the connections that truly benefit both parties.

18.12 Digital Tools for Building Connections

In modern times, the internet can expand your reach. While it cannot replace face-to-face friendship, digital platforms can help you connect with others who share your goals or challenges.

- **Online Forums**: Specialized forums or social media groups exist for nearly every interest—fitness, writing, business start-ups, and more.
- **Video Calls**: If distance separates you from old friends or family, set up regular calls. Even a short conversation can maintain closeness.
- **Networking Apps**: Professional platforms let you engage with people in your industry, ask for advice, or find events.
- **Shared Project Spaces**: If you collaborate on a hobby or volunteer effort, use online tools to keep everyone on the same page and build camaraderie.

Though virtual, these ties can still be meaningful, especially if you eventually get opportunities to meet in person or work on joint ventures.

18.13 Maintaining Bonds Across Busy Lives

Even good friends can drift apart if life gets hectic. To keep bonds strong:

- **Plan Ahead**: Schedule a monthly coffee date or phone call. Write it on your calendar so it does not slip away among other obligations.
- **Use Quick Check-Ins**: Send a short text or voice note when you are thinking of someone. Let them know you care, even if you do not have time for a full conversation.
- **Celebrate Achievements**: When you hear good news about a friend or mentor, congratulate them. If they share bad news, offer a few encouraging words.
- **Adapt to New Chapters**: If someone moves, changes careers, or has a child, your friendship might look different. Stay flexible and find ways to connect that match the new reality.

Consistency in small actions can keep relationships thriving despite distance or busy schedules.

18.14 Building a Network at Work

For many men, work is where they spend most hours. Building supportive relationships there can enhance job satisfaction and open doors to collaboration and mentorship. However, boundaries matter—some topics are best kept private to maintain professionalism.

- **Offer Help**: If you see a coworker struggling with a skill you have, step in or give tips. Generosity often breeds reciprocity.
- **Respect Personal Space**: Not everyone wants deep friendships at work, so watch for cues. Start with casual chat about shared interests before diving into personal matters.
- **Arrange Lunches or Breaks**: Invite a colleague to lunch or a short walk outside. These small events build trust beyond official meetings.
- **Manage Conflicts Politely**: If disagreements arise, handle them calmly and fairly. Avoid gossip or personal attacks, as that can destroy a supportive environment.

A network at work can make your days more enjoyable and less stressful, knowing you have allies in your professional sphere.

18.15 Combining Social Events with Shared Aims

Sometimes you can form a network almost effortlessly by centering it around a mutual objective. For example:

- **Start a Reading Circle**: If you want to read more about personal development or any topic, invite a few interested friends or coworkers. Rotate book choices and meet monthly.
- **Fitness Challenges**: Gather a group to track daily steps or plan weekly workouts. Everyone motivates each other to stay active.
- **Skill-Sharing Nights**: If you and your friends have different talents, rotate who teaches a mini-class. One friend might show basic guitar, another might demonstrate cooking tips, and so on.
- **Group Volunteering**: Pick a local cause—like a food drive or park cleanup—and involve friends or colleagues. Serving together builds camaraderie.

These joint ventures produce a support network naturally, as you regularly bond over an engaging activity or goal.

18.16 Family as Part of Your Network

Family can be a complicated source of help, especially if there are old conflicts or differences in values. However, family ties often stand strong in tough situations. Recognizing how to involve relatives in your support circle can be beneficial:

- **Identify Safe Topics**: If your relationship with certain family members is tense, focus on areas where you connect well or can help each other.
- **Set Boundaries for Conflicts**: Family gatherings can bring up old grudges. Kindly but firmly steer the conversation away from sensitive subjects if needed.
- **Ask for Specific Help**: If you need a hand with a home project or babysitting, family might be more willing than you expect, as long as you approach them respectfully.
- **Stay Neutral**: If there is tension between different relatives, try not to get sucked into the middle. Support them individually without fueling feuds.

When managed thoughtfully, family can be a powerful part of your network—offering emotional grounding and practical assistance.

18.17 Overcoming Social Anxiety

Some men want a support network but find social interactions nerve-racking. Feeling anxious in crowds or meeting new people is more common than you might think. Try these steps:

- **Start Small**: Challenge yourself with brief or low-pressure social events, like chatting with one new coworker at lunch.
- **Prepare Topics**: Think of a few simple conversation starters—questions about hobbies, local news, or events.
- **Focus on Others**: Shifting attention to learning about the other person can reduce your own worry. People generally like to talk about themselves if asked kindly.
- **Practice Self-Calming Techniques**: If you feel anxious, use slow breathing or grounding methods. Remind yourself you do not have to be perfect—just sincere.

With each positive interaction, your confidence can grow, making it easier to expand your circle.

18.18 Online Boundaries and Caution

While the internet is a powerful tool for forming connections, be mindful:

- **Privacy**: Limit how much personal information you share publicly. Avoid giving out addresses or financial details early on.
- **Verify Identities**: Some people misrepresent themselves online. If a friendship grows serious, try to meet in safe, public places.
- **Balanced Screen Time**: Spend enough face-to-face time with local contacts or offline activities so you are not solely relying on virtual interaction.
- **Report Harmful Behavior**: If someone harasses or threatens you, use the platform's blocking/reporting features. Your safety is paramount.

Staying cautious prevents negative experiences from overshadowing the benefits of online connections.

18.19 Long-Term Maintenance of a Support System

Building a network is one step; keeping it vibrant is another. People move, change jobs, or have life shifts. How do you ensure your support system remains steady?

- **Adapt**: If close friends relocate, find ways to stay in touch through calls or occasional visits. Also stay open to forming new local ties.
- **Offer Help Without Being Asked**: Sometimes friends are hesitant to ask for assistance. Noticing their struggles and volunteering help can keep your bond active.
- **Stay Positive**: Constant negativity can push people away. Share honest concerns, but also bring optimism or solutions when possible.
- **Evaluate Your Needs**: As your life changes, you may need different forms of support or encounter new groups that match your evolving interests.

By checking in periodically—both with your connections and with yourself—you keep your network relevant and effective for your current phase of life.

18.20 Conclusion of Chapter 18

Creating a support network is not about clinging to others out of weakness; it is about recognizing that human connections can enrich your journey through life. Friends, family, mentors, and professional helpers can all be part of the system that supports your goals, mental health, and overall stability. In return, you offer genuine friendship, assistance, and empathy, making the bond stronger and beneficial for everyone involved.

Men who accept the value of a supportive circle often discover that challenges become more manageable, triumphs become sweeter when shared, and personal growth is accelerated by the wisdom and encouragement of others. As we continue to Chapters 19 and 20—covering long-term plans for well-being and concluding thoughts—you will see how your network can be a crucial pillar for sustaining the improvements you have worked so hard to build throughout these chapters. Having reliable people around you ensures you do not face life's demands alone, preserving both your sense of self and your connections with those who matter.

CHAPTER 19

Long-Term Plans for Well-Being

Introduction
Building healthy habits and a positive mindset is not a one-time task. It is an ongoing process that can shift as life moves through different stages. Men who set their sights on long-term wellness are more likely to maintain the improvements gained so far—like steady self-respect, balanced relationships, and the ability to handle stress. This chapter looks at how to craft a plan for the future, tying together the key lessons from earlier chapters. By doing so, you set yourself on a sustainable course.

You will explore why long-term goals are different from short-term achievements, and how to adapt your strategies as you age or face unexpected changes. We will also discuss common obstacles—like setbacks, routine fatigue, or changing priorities—and how to manage them effectively. By the end, you will have tools for staying consistent over years, not just weeks or months.

19.1 The Nature of Long-Term Thinking

When people talk about looking far ahead, they often imagine detailed maps of their future. However, life rarely goes precisely according to plan. Rather than creating a rigid blueprint, long-term thinking is more about identifying directions or themes you wish to maintain—like continual self-improvement, mental and physical health, strong bonds, and fulfilling work. Your goals can still have targets and deadlines, but they should come with a willingness to adjust when life throws unexpected curves.

- **Steering vs. Controlling**: Imagine guiding a boat at sea. You can pick a direction and steer, but storms might force temporary detours. You do not abandon your aim, but you adapt.
- **Focus on Habits and Values**: Rather than obsessing over one outcome, build routines and decide on core principles that keep you steady. For instance, commit to being honest, or to exercising weekly, or to family dinners whenever possible.
- **Check Your Compass**: Every so often, reflect on whether you are still living by your chosen principles. If not, realign your daily actions.

By seeing the future in terms of ongoing directions, you can avoid the frustration that arises when every detail does not go exactly as imagined.

19.2 Consolidating Good Habits

One big key to long-term progress is locking in the positive routines you have built, so they become second nature. Consistency matters more than occasional bursts of effort.

- **Spot Your Core Routines**: Think about which habits have helped you the most—maybe daily exercise, a weekly check-in with a support partner, or journaling each evening.
- **Reinforce Them**: Continue using reminders if needed, like phone alerts or sticky notes. If you find yourself slipping, return to the habit as soon as you notice.
- **Evolve as Needed**: A habit might need tweaking if your schedule changes, like shifting from morning runs to evening runs when your job hours shift. The key is to keep the essence of the habit alive.
- **Reward System**: Let yourself acknowledge each time you follow your habit. These mini-satisfactions help lock in the routine.

Stable habits function like pillars supporting your day-to-day life. If your schedule or environment shifts, keep the pillar in place by adjusting only its form, not discarding it.

19.3 Financial Health and Security

Men often overlook the role of financial stability in overall well-being. Money problems can lead to stress, conflict at home, or lack of freedom to pursue interests. Planning finances responsibly can remove many pressures and allow you to remain on track for the other goals in this book.

- **Create a Simple Budget**: List your monthly income and expenses. Track how much you spend on necessities, savings, and leisure. Aim to spend less than you earn so you can save for rainy days or future plans.

- **Tackle Debt Carefully**: High-interest debts, like credit card balances, can weigh you down. Focus on paying these off steadily while avoiding extra charges.
- **Plan for Future Goals**: Whether it is a home purchase, children's education, or starting a business, set aside regular amounts in a dedicated account if possible.
- **Learn Basic Investing**: Consider low-risk options, such as broad market index funds or secure savings tools. You do not have to be a finance expert, but some basic knowledge can protect your money.
- **Seek Advice**: If your finances are complex, speak with a financial advisor. Just as with mental health or fitness, professional guidance can prevent costly mistakes.

Being mindful of money removes a major source of anxiety, helping you keep a balanced mind and the freedom to make choices that align with your values.

19.4 Regular Health Checkups and Maintenance

Physical health is easy to ignore when everything seems fine. However, small issues can grow over time if not caught early. Scheduling checkups and practicing preventive care can protect you from health crises that derail all other plans.

- **Routine Doctor Visits**: An annual exam (or as recommended) can spot potential problems before they worsen.
- **Dental Care**: Regular cleanings and checkups prevent painful and expensive treatments later.
- **Eye and Ear Checks**: Vision and hearing change gradually. Testing them can preserve these senses for the long haul.
- **Mental Health Screenings**: Some clinics offer screenings or questionnaires for depression, anxiety, and other conditions. Even if you feel okay, an occasional check can ensure you are not missing subtle signs.
- **Fitness Upkeep**: Maintain a baseline of activity. If you built a certain strength or endurance level, keep it by exercising regularly.

By treating health as a continuous priority, you reduce the chance that an avoidable condition will knock you off your path.

19.5 Periodic Life Audits

Change is inevitable. A job may become unfulfilling, relationships might shift, or personal goals can evolve. A "life audit" is a structured way to see if your current actions match your deepest interests and whether adjustments are needed.

1. **Schedule It**: Choose a frequency—every six months or annually. Make a quiet afternoon for reflecting on the past period.
2. **Check Core Areas**: Inspect health, relationships, finances, personal growth, and sense of purpose.
3. **Ask Key Questions**: "Am I still happy with my job?" "Do I feel close to my loved ones?" "Am I learning new things or stuck in place?"
4. **Plan Next Steps**: If you find mismatches, write down some ideas on how to fix them. Maybe you will explore a new side gig or plan more regular visits with friends.

Routine life audits help you catch simmering dissatisfaction before it turns into bigger problems.

19.6 Handling Relapses and Setbacks

No matter how well you prepare, setbacks happen—an injury might stop your exercise routine, a lapse in budgeting might cause a financial hiccup, or negative emotions could resurface after a conflict at home. The difference between a short stumble and a permanent backslide often lies in your response.

- **Stay Calm**: It is normal to feel frustrated or disappointed at a setback, but avoid spiraling into harsh self-blame.
- **Assess What Went Wrong**: Did you push too hard too soon? Did you ignore certain warning signs? Identifying causes reduces the chance of repeating the same mistake.
- **Reinforce Your Habits**: Return to your established routines as soon as possible. Even if you are not at the same level, the structure will help rebuild momentum.
- **Seek Extra Support**: If the setback is big, talk to a mentor, a support partner, or a counselor. Outside perspectives can remind you that one mistake does not erase the good progress made.

- **Learn and Move Forward**: Each setback can teach you how to handle future issues more effectively.

Accepting that slips are part of a long process can help you maintain a stable, self-respecting approach even in tough moments.

19.7 Updating Goals Over Time

Your dreams at 25 might not be the same at 45 or 65. Perhaps you chose a career path that felt right in your early years but now want something else. Or you might want a different style of living that better fits your current family situation. Being willing to update or replace goals is a natural part of maturity.

- **Check If a Goal Still Resonates**: Ask if the excitement or reason behind it still holds. If not, it might be time to revise.
- **Plan Transitions Carefully**: If you need to change careers, finances, or location, do some research and create a step-by-step approach.
- **Balance Risk with Realism**: Make sure your new direction is feasible. If it is a big leap, prepare with knowledge, savings, or a trial run if possible.
- **Stay True to Values**: The most satisfying goals align with your personal code—like helping others, being creative, or gaining freedom in your schedule.

This flexibility keeps you from feeling trapped or from clinging to plans that no longer serve you.

19.8 Keeping Relationships Alive and Growing

Earlier chapters discussed healthy relationships and building support. Long-term well-being also depends on regularly nurturing those bonds so they do not wither.

- **Adapt Communication**: As years pass, new technologies or job demands might alter how often you can see friends or family. Adjust your communication style while keeping the bond.
- **Celebrate Milestones**: If a friend or family member reaches a big step in life—like a new job or a new addition to the family—recognize it. This effort keeps the friendship strong.

- **Revisit Roles**: People change. Parents age and may need help. Children become adults who want to be treated with respect and independence. Partners develop new interests. Be open to shifting dynamics.
- **Maintain Clear Boundaries**: As life evolves, so can demands on your time. Knowing when to say "no" or discuss new limits ensures you do not become overstretched.

Constant adjustments keep relationships healthy and relevant as each person grows in different ways.

19.9 Sustaining Self-Respect

Self-respect, discussed in Chapter 1, must be revisited regularly. Life events—like layoffs, breakups, or unexpected failures—can shake your sense of worth. Keep building that inner foundation:

- **Speak Kindly to Yourself**: Keep an eye on negative self-talk. Use balanced statements that acknowledge mistakes but also recognize strengths.
- **Acknowledge Achievements**: No matter how small, each positive move counts. You might keep a log of completed goals or good deeds.
- **Stand by Your Principles**: If you value honesty, fairness, or kindness, act on those values even when tempted to do otherwise. Living up to your own standards boosts self-respect.
- **Forgive Mistakes**: Letting go of self-blame is crucial. Learn what you can, then allow yourself to move on.

A man with stable self-respect is less likely to compromise his well-being or chase external validation at the cost of personal authenticity.

19.10 Mentoring Others

A beneficial way to maintain your own growth is by guiding those who are behind you on a similar path. Whether it is younger coworkers, friends new to a skill, or family members, offering mentorship can reinforce your own lessons.

- **Deepen Your Knowledge**: Explaining concepts or demonstrating skills clarifies your understanding and uncovers gaps you might not have noticed.
- **Boost Confidence**: Helping others succeed is rewarding and builds a sense of capability.
- **Give Balanced Help**: Avoid taking over their tasks. Offer pointers or share experiences so they can develop independence.
- **Stay Humble**: Mentorship is not about showing off expertise. It is about guiding someone in a way that respects their unique process.

By teaching, you remind yourself of the key habits, mindsets, and coping strategies that brought you this far. It is a living way to keep your progress alive.

19.11 Maintaining a Growth Mindset

A "growth mindset" means believing you can improve through effort, learning, and adaptation. It contrasts with a "fixed mindset," which assumes your abilities or traits are mostly unchangeable. Over the long term, a growth mindset sustains motivation to keep learning and evolving.

- **View Challenges as Learning**: Each obstacle is a chance to sharpen your skills or gain new perspectives.
- **Embrace Adaptation**: Accept that you will not stay the same person you are today. Change can be beneficial if guided by your values and willingness to learn.
- **Seek Feedback**: Constructive critiques from friends, mentors, or coworkers can reveal blind spots. A growth-oriented person uses feedback for improvement rather than feeling attacked.
- **Stay Curious**: New fields, hobbies, or interactions can spark fresh inspiration even later in life.

Staying open to what you do not yet know protects you from stagnation, ensuring that you continue to expand your horizons.

19.12 Expanding Your Comfort Zone Gradually

Long-term plans often involve stepping beyond what feels safe. Whether it is trying new career paths, traveling to different environments, or taking on unfamiliar responsibilities, gradual expansion is more sustainable than drastic leaps.

1. **Identify a Mild Challenge**: Something that stretches you but is not terrifying—like speaking up more in work meetings, or trying a new group activity.
2. **Take Small Steps**: If public speaking is your goal, start with a short presentation to a small team, then build to bigger audiences.
3. **Celebrate Each Step**: Recognize every time you push beyond your usual limits. This positive reinforcement encourages you to keep going.
4. **Review and Adjust**: If a particular step feels too daunting, scale it down rather than quitting entirely.

Consistent mild challenges over months or years can lead to surprising transformations in skill, confidence, and life options.

19.13 Passing Down Values and Lessons

Men often think about their legacy—what they leave behind for children, younger relatives, or the broader community. Part of long-term well-being is ensuring your knowledge, ethics, and experiences help the next generation.

- **Family Conversations**: If you have children, share stories of how you overcame obstacles. Use real examples so they see how lessons apply in real life.
- **Public Contributions**: Write articles, create videos, or speak at local events about topics you have mastered. This can help others beyond your immediate circle.
- **Volunteer Mentorship**: Youth programs, community centers, or online platforms can connect you with young people who need guidance.
- **Model Good Behavior**: Even if you do not say much, living out your principles can teach by example. People who watch you handle stress or treat others fairly might be inspired.

By actively passing on what you have learned, you link your current progress to a larger sense of purpose.

19.14 Handling Major Life Transitions

Big changes—like retirement, becoming a parent, losing a loved one, or relocating—can shake your routines. These events might challenge your self-identity or hamper your usual habits. Approaching transitions with thoughtful planning can maintain your sense of stability.

- **Plan Early When Possible**: If you know retirement is coming, gradually shift into new interests or part-time work to fill your day. If you are moving, research the new community to find potential friends or resources.
- **Accept Emotional Phases**: Transitions can bring sadness, excitement, or anxiety. Recognize these feelings as part of the process, rather than ignoring them.
- **Rely on Support**: Use your network, family, or counselors to talk through concerns. External perspectives can help you navigate the emotional mix.
- **Keep Core Habits**: If you always journal in the morning, continue doing so even if you move or switch jobs. Familiar routines can give a sense of consistency.

Life transitions do not have to halt your progress. With proactive steps, they can even open new avenues for growth.

19.15 Protecting Mental Health Over the Long Haul

Mental wellness is as essential as physical health, especially as the years go by. Without consistent attention, stress, anxiety, or depression can creep up again.

- **Keep Check-In Methods**: Regularly ask yourself how you are feeling emotionally. If you notice signs of sadness, anger, or indifference lasting weeks, do not wait—seek help.
- **Balance Stimulation and Rest**: The mind needs both activity (learning, social engagement, problem-solving) and rest (mindfulness, breaks from digital bombardment).

- **Avoid Isolation**: Life changes like job loss or retirement can shrink your social circle. Make an effort to stay connected or build new friendships.
- **Stay Engaged**: Find some project or hobby that gives you a sense of purpose. When people lose meaning in daily life, mental health often suffers.

Ongoing mental health care sets the foundation for all other aspects of well-being to thrive.

19.16 Using Reflection to Stay on Course

Earlier chapters introduced reflection as a way to process daily life. Long-term, you can turn reflection into a guiding practice.

- **Monthly or Quarterly Reviews**: Look back at your major tasks, emotional highs and lows, and what caused them.
- **Track Patterns**: Maybe you notice that winter months affect your mood or that big deadlines cause you to skip exercise. These observations let you plan better.
- **Set Next Objectives**: Choose a small focus for the next month, like improving your morning routine or contacting an old friend. Reflection leads naturally to action.
- **Stay Open**: Reflection is only useful if you are willing to acknowledge where you fell short and take steps to fix it.

By integrating reflection into your ongoing plan, you ensure constant alignment between your actions and your deeper goals.

19.17 Recognizing the Value of Contentment

Sometimes, men chase endless improvement without ever taking a moment to enjoy where they are. While growth is crucial, contentment is also a valid part of long-term well-being. Recognizing your present blessings and achievements can prevent burnout.

- **Practice Gratitude**: Spend a little time each day noting what went right—whether it is a decent meal, a kind word from a friend, or a completed task at work.
- **Avoid Endless Comparison**: Checking yourself against others' achievements can create unnecessary pressure. Compare your current self only to your past self.
- **Allow Relaxation**: Realize it is okay to have moments where you are not hustling or improving—just living. That sense of being at ease supports mental calm and recharges you for the next challenge.
- **Stay Balanced**: Contentment does not mean giving up on future goals. It just means you are not in a constant rush, and you appreciate the now as well.

Men who find healthy contentment tend to make better decisions, free from the desperation or envy that can arise in a relentless pursuit of more.

19.18 Making Room for Fun and Experimentation

A plan for lasting well-being should not be purely about discipline and routine. Fun, humor, and occasional spontaneity also help you stay energized. Experimenting with new experiences or hobbies can keep life fresh.

- **Try Something New Regularly**: Whether it is a new recipe or a free workshop in town, novelty keeps the brain engaged.
- **Embrace Humor**: Sharing laughs with friends, watching comedic shows, or finding something funny in daily struggles can lighten stress.
- **Plan "Random Days"**: Once in a while, let yourself explore the city with no fixed agenda or pick a random item from a hobby store to try.
- **Balance with Routine**: You do not want chaos in your schedule, but a dash of unpredictability can break monotony and remind you that life can be enjoyable.

Fun is not a waste of time; it is part of emotional health, fueling a mindset that can tackle responsibilities with renewed spirit.

19.19 Contributing to Society

As men build themselves up, many feel a desire to give back. This might involve volunteering, community projects, or activism for causes that matter to you. Being part of something larger than your personal bubble can bring a sense of direction and pride.

- **Volunteer Locally**: From food banks to youth mentorship, local activities can make a clear impact on your neighborhood.
- **Share Expertise**: If you are skilled in a certain area—like writing, coding, or art—consider donating your services to nonprofit groups.
- **Participate in Local Issues**: Attend town meetings or join committees that shape community policies.
- **Teach Future Generations**: Offer free workshops to children or teenagers, passing on practical knowledge they can use.

Contributing beyond your immediate circle can deepen your sense of purpose, keep you grounded, and connect you with like-minded individuals.

19.20 Conclusion of Chapter 19

Long-term well-being is not about aiming for a moment of perfection and then stopping. It is an ongoing effort to maintain health, meaningful relationships, personal growth, and a stable sense of self-respect. By consolidating good habits, preparing for change, and staying open to new possibilities, men can carry forward the gains made in earlier chapters.

Your plan should remain flexible, reflecting that life rarely follows a straight path. A strong foundation of values, healthy routines, and supportive connections will keep you steady in the face of setbacks or transitions. Whether in career, family life, or personal growth, you can continue evolving without losing your grounding. In the final chapter, we will wrap up the entire book, offering concluding thoughts on how to remain strong and caring toward yourself. This sets the stage for a life where self-respect, emotional health, and good relationships serve as the backbone for any future goals.

CHAPTER 20

Conclusion and Final Thoughts

Introduction
You have reached the final chapter of this book, which brings together the core messages from all previous sections. We have covered the meaning of self-respect, how to break limiting beliefs, creating positive thought patterns, building emotional resilience, balancing personal needs with external responsibilities, and finding motivation and support for the long run. These topics, although varied, all connect to one essential principle: a man who looks after both his mental and physical well-being is better able to show kindness to himself and to others.

In these closing pages, we will revisit the major themes and discuss how they form an ongoing approach to life rather than a one-time fix. We will also mention simple ways to keep these ideas alive in daily routines. By reflecting on what you have learned, you can craft a personalized way of living that respects both your individual worth and the value of the people around you.

20.1 Reviewing Key Themes from Each Chapter

The chapters in this book built on one another, each focusing on a different aspect of self-care and personal development:

1. **Self Respect**: Recognizing your own worth is not vanity. It lays the groundwork for balanced living.
2. **Breaking Old Beliefs**: Unlearning harmful ideas picked up over the years frees you to grow without outdated baggage.
3. **Positive Thoughts for Daily Life**: Simple techniques, like daily reflections and focusing on solutions, create a healthier mindset.
4. **Building Inner Strength**: True resilience involves discipline, core values, and an honest look at personal weaknesses.
5. **Handling Emotional Pain**: Accepting and managing deep feelings safely can prevent long-term harm.
6. **Discovering Personal Interests**: Finding new outlets boosts mental vitality and forms positive escapes from stress.

7. **Tactics for a Healthy Lifestyle**: Balanced nutrition, regular activity, and mindful choices support both body and mind.
8. **True Friendships and Connection**: Real bonds require trust, open communication, and a willingness to share burdens.
9. **Building a Productive Mindset**: Clear goals, time management, and smart routines can lead to more efficient use of energy.
10. **Skills for Good Communication**: Speaking and listening with honesty and respect form the foundation for strong relationships.
11. **Managing Conflict at Work and Home**: Constructive methods can keep disagreements from exploding into lasting damage.
12. **Overcoming Shame and Guilt**: Letting go of harmful self-blame makes room for healing and renewed self-worth.
13. **Achieving Personal Goals**: Breaking big aims into manageable steps and tracking progress is key to steady success.
14. **Growth Through Reflection**: Regularly looking inward offers insights that keep you aligned with your core values.
15. **Practical Ways to Find Motivation**: Tying tasks to deeper meaning, using daily "wins," and forming encouraging environments can sustain energy.
16. **Handling Stress Without Harm**: A mix of quick fixes and long-term habits can keep tension at a safe level.
17. **Balancing Personal Needs and Relationships**: Setting boundaries and communicating clearly helps maintain harmony between your wants and those of loved ones.
18. **Creating a Support Network**: Reliable friends, mentors, and community ties offer stability through life's ups and downs.
19. **Long-Term Plans for Well-Being**: Keeping good habits, staying open to adaptation, and nurturing relationships over the years results in lasting stability.

Each piece of the puzzle helps form a well-rounded, healthy approach, but the real power lies in how you combine them day by day.

20.2 Creating a Custom Checklist

Not every point in this book will apply equally to every man. You might already excel in certain areas while needing more work in others. Consider writing a short checklist that highlights the chapters or lessons most relevant to you:

- **Identify Three Priority Areas**: Maybe emotional pain management, building a support network, and stress control are your biggest challenges.
- **Note One Action per Topic**: For emotional pain, perhaps a daily journal. For the support network, plan monthly meetups with a friend. For stress, commit to short breathing exercises at lunchtime.
- **Check In Weekly**: Look at your personal list. Did you follow through? How did it feel? Adjust if something is not working.

This custom approach helps you translate general advice into specific, tangible steps that fit your life.

20.3 Staying Flexible in Implementation

Even if you start strong, life circumstances can alter your ability to maintain all routines perfectly. Children's schedules, job transitions, health shifts—these can disrupt your best plans. Flexibility is key.

- **Adapt Timelines**: If you cannot do a 30-minute workout every day, try 15 minutes or switch to short walks at work.
- **Blend Activities**: Turn chores into mini-workouts or family bonding time. Listen to uplifting talks while driving.
- **Revisit Methods**: If an approach feels stale, try a new angle. For instance, if journaling every night becomes dull, switch to voice notes on your phone or a weekly summary format.
- **Stay Alert to Burnout**: If you feel overly pressured by your plan, reduce the intensity. It is better to do a moderate amount consistently than to overextend and quit.

Adapting prevents you from getting stuck in all-or-nothing thinking.

20.4 The Role of Self-Compassion

Many men push themselves relentlessly while offering others understanding. If you beat yourself up for every slip, you might lose morale or revert to old harmful habits. Self-compassion is the act of treating yourself with the same sympathy you would give a close friend.

- **Acknowledge Your Limits**: Humans have emotional and physical limits. Pushing beyond them consistently leads to breakdowns.
- **View Mistakes Calmly**: Instead of labeling yourself "lazy" or "unworthy," say, "I made a misstep, but that does not define me."
- **Encourage Yourself**: Simple phrases like, "I can learn from this," or "I am improving bit by bit" can keep negative self-criticism in check.
- **Separate Behavior from Identity**: Failing at a task is not the same as being a failure as a person.

Self-compassion does not mean lowering standards; it means cultivating a supportive internal environment that fosters resilience and steady growth.

20.5 Recognizing the Need for Support at Any Stage

Some men assume that once they reach a certain level of success or maturity, they should manage everything alone. But even the most accomplished person can benefit from friendships, guidance, or a caring family circle.

- **Mentors and Peers**: You can be successful at work yet still gain insights from someone who has dealt with a different set of life challenges.
- **Emotional Anchors**: A partner, friend, or family member who truly listens can help you make sense of problems faster than you would on your own.
- **Professional Guidance**: Therapists, coaches, or financial advisors are not just for when you are in crisis. They can guide you to even higher levels of well-being or performance.

No matter how far you have come, do not hesitate to seek support if you sense you could benefit from it.

20.6 Balancing Acceptance and Ambition

This book has encouraged both self-improvement and self-acceptance. These are not contradictory. Accepting yourself—your strengths, flaws, and unique traits—helps you build a secure base from which you can strive for better outcomes without harsh self-judgment.

- **Avoid the Perfection Trap**: Ambition turns toxic if you see every imperfection as a catastrophe. Recognize that improvement is a path, not an end point.
- **Value the Present Moment**: Even as you chase future goals, do not miss the daily joys or small successes happening now.
- **Use Mistakes as Information**: They are signals about what to adjust, not proof that you are a lost cause.
- **Balance External Goals with Inner Peace**: Achievements should enhance your life, not dominate it.

By blending acceptance and ambition, you can keep moving forward without losing your mental balance.

20.7 Revisiting Foundational Values

Throughout these chapters, the subject of values came up often—principles like honesty, loyalty, kindness, or fairness that shape how you act. Keeping these in mind as you plan or make decisions is vital for consistency.

- **Live by Your Code**: If honesty is central, remain honest in small matters as well as major ones. If fairness is key, treat people fairly even when no one is watching.
- **Prevent Regrets**: Acting against your values for short-term gain often leads to deeper regrets.
- **Stay Aware of Contradictions**: If you notice tension between your goals and your values, adapt the goal or your approach so they align better.
- **Reassess Periodically**: Values may mature or shift in priority. Keep them updated so they reflect your latest sense of what is important.

Values serve as an internal compass, preventing you from drifting too far off-track when external pressures mount.

20.8 Making Small Positive Impacts Daily

A grand plan for personal growth might be inspiring, but the real progress often occurs in ordinary moments—small choices repeated over time.

- **Tiny Acts of Kindness**: Open a door for someone, send a supportive note, or give a quick thank-you to a coworker. These habits foster a positive outlook.
- **Micro-Habits**: A single push-up, one glass of water, or a two-minute cleanup might seem trivial. Yet each mini-step leads to a cleaner, healthier, or more ordered life when done consistently.
- **Regular Emotional Check-Ins**: Take a second to note your mood. If you feel a bit off, do a calming activity or share a quick message with a friend.
- **Pay Attention**: Notice your environment—nature, people's expressions, small details. Being present helps you appreciate life's simple gifts.

Incremental efforts not only add up but also keep you engaged with the world in a mindful way.

20.9 Embracing Change as a Permanent Condition

Though we avoid certain words, we can acknowledge that life is a constant flow. The strategies in this book do not promise a static result. Instead, they equip you to handle the evolving nature of your existence. A change in career, family structure, or personal outlook might shift your priorities tomorrow or next year.

- **Stay Curious About What's Next**: Each change can be an opportunity to discover new capacities within yourself or form new relationships.
- **Reflect on Past Adaptations**: Looking back at how you handled previous changes builds confidence for future ones.
- **Keep Your Tools Handy**: The ideas here—like reflection, communication, stress management, boundary-setting—are universal skills. You can apply them to fresh situations even if the context is brand-new.
- **Allow Growth in Identity**: Your sense of self is not frozen. Be ready to welcome new roles or sides of your personality as they reveal themselves.

Accepting ongoing change prevents frustration when life does not stay exactly as it is now.

20.10 Contributing to a Healthier Culture

Men's well-being does not develop in isolation—it interacts with social expectations and cultural norms. By applying the lessons from this book, you can also make your environment more supportive for other men who may struggle with rigid standards of masculinity or feel unsafe voicing emotional concerns.

- **Model Openness**: If you show calm confidence in addressing personal emotions or asking for help, others may realize it is acceptable to do the same.
- **Encourage Communication**: If you see a friend withdrawing, initiate a conversation. Even a simple check-in like "How are you really doing?" can open doors.
- **Challenge Unhelpful Stereotypes**: If your social group mocks vulnerability or views mental health care as weakness, politely counter with a fact or personal story.
- **Build Inclusive Groups**: When organizing events—like game nights or group workouts—be welcoming of varied personalities and skill levels.

By living these principles outwardly, you not only boost your own life, but help shift the broader climate in a more supportive direction.

20.11 A Final Word on Patience

One thread woven through the entire book is patience—patience with yourself and with others. True transformation rarely happens overnight. Even if your efforts feel slow or you stumble, perseverance yields results:

- **Stay Motivated**: Keep your bigger reasons in mind, whether it is your health, family, or personal fulfillment.
- **Accept Gradual Gains**: Small improvements daily or weekly accumulate into substantial progress over a year or longer.
- **Forgive Delays**: Life might pause your advancement at times, but that is not a permanent stop unless you choose to quit.
- **Acknowledge Milestones**: While avoiding certain celebratory words, you can still mark small wins as evidence that you are on the right track.

Patience is the steady breath that keeps you going through distractions and trials, ensuring you do not give up after a short burst of enthusiasm.

20.12 Your Ongoing Journey Begins Now

We end by emphasizing that this entire process is not a "one and done" event. The ideas in these 20 chapters form a toolkit you can return to and adapt. Some sections will resonate more at different stages—maybe you will return to chapters on conflict resolution when faced with a job crisis, or revisit the part on goal-setting when you decide to learn a new skill at 50.

What matters is that you keep these resources in mind as you continue living. Use them whenever you sense you are drifting from your values, neglecting self-care, or needing to re-center yourself. This dynamic approach allows you to thrive in changing circumstances without losing the core of who you are.

20.13 Immediate Next Steps

If you are not sure how to proceed right now, here are a few suggestions:

1. **Pick One Area**: From the chapters that spoke to you the most, identify a single topic to focus on (like self-talk or boundary-setting).
2. **Implement One Action This Week**: For instance, spend 10 minutes journaling each evening, or schedule a call with an old friend.
3. **Review After One Month**: Check if you see any positive shifts—less stress, better mood, small progress on a hobby or personal goal.
4. **Adjust or Add Another Step**: If the initial action works, keep it and consider adding a second habit. If not, modify it.

Starting small wards off overwhelm and builds momentum.

20.14 Expressing Gratitude

While certain words are avoided, you can still express thanks for the people, experiences, and resources that help you along. This can be a quiet, personal practice or an active gesture toward those who have been supportive. Gratefulness keeps you aware that you do not travel alone and that even in tough times, some good elements exist in your world.

20.15 Conclusion of Chapter 20 and the Book

This final chapter weaves together all the threads discussed before—self-respect, healthy beliefs, positive thoughts, emotional resilience, communication skills, motivation, stress management, balanced relationships, and long-term strategies for stability. The main point is that you can steadily become a man who respects himself in a genuine way, cares for his body and mind, and builds solid, respectful relationships. This type of man is not flawless, but he has the tools to grow from mistakes and keep going despite hardships.

With these 20 chapters in hand, you have a structured framework for dealing with the many facets of life: mental well-being, self-improvement, connections with others, and overall balance. The real task is putting them into practice. No outside authority can impose these principles on you; you must choose to use them daily or weekly in ways that fit your personal life. Whether you are taking the first step toward self-respect or refreshing your approach after years of experience, the material here can support you.

As you close this book, remember that no one chapter holds all the answers. It is your willingness to continually refine and combine these lessons that will yield real results. Keep learning, keep adapting, and keep valuing your unique worth. From this point on, the story is yours to write—supported by the knowledge that you have every right to treat yourself with fairness, embrace your good qualities, and strive for a life that honors both your personal self and the people who share your path.

www.ingramcontent.com/pod-product-compliance
Lightning Source LLC
LaVergne TN
LVHW012103070526
838202LV00056B/5604